"Many business men have pr⋯⋯⋯⋯⋯⋯⋯⋯ e-
dominately African Americ⋯ ⋯⋯ ⋯⋯⋯ ⋯⋯⋯⋯ty.
Tom is one of the few who has given much more than
received. Nixland is proof that businesses and business
people can profit greatly while giving back much more
than received, to the people they serve."
—Rev. Jerrold T. Smith, CEO
1 Plus One Management Inc.

"An entertaining read that captures the evolution of a
family business into an industry leader and champion for
doing business the right way for the underprivileged."
—David J. Iannini, CEO,
William & Henry Associates, Investment Bankers

"For over 40 years I have had the pleasure of working beside
Tom Nix sharing "The Great Adventure" of building Nix
Check Cashing. As a leader with unwavering principals
and integrity, he inspires his family, friends, employees
and community. Tom developed a business strategy that
provided not only financial services to the underserved
community of Southern California, but also fought hard
for legislation that protected both the industry and consumer rights. Recognizing challenges in the community
and having a strong desire to address them, Tom hired
from the communities we serve and developed relationships with community leaders creating events such as our

annual food drive, scholarship program, and an anti-gang program. NIXLAND gives the reader a unique view of Tom and what it took to run a successful business in the inner city of Los Angeles."

—Darline Gavin, former Sr. Vice President, Nix Check Cashing

"I, Dr. Sweet Alice Harris, am the founder and the executive director of The Parents of Watts Working with the Youth and Adults Inc. It has been a non-profit organization for 46 years. I have lived here in the Watts community myself for 60 years. I have known Mr. Tom Nix and worked with him for the community of Watts for 30 years. We have benefitted from his business "Nix Check Cashing". Our neighbors here in the Watts community would have not made it. Our children would have not finished school and gone on to college if it wasn't for the amazing help of Mr. Nix. His gracious amount of help, dedication, time, money and his family have all been donated to the community of Watts. He has also provided employment for the community of Watts. I have always said and will say now, "God bless Mr. Nix and his family for keeping us so close to the Nix family."

—Dr. Sweet Alice Harris, Executive Director & Founder, The Parents of Watts Working with the Youth and Adults Inc.

NIXLAND

My Wild Ride in the Inner City
Check Cashing Industry

──────────┼──────────

TOM NIX

Founder of Nix Check Cashing

BusinessGhost Books
Irvine, CA

For more information contact:
tomnix@nixland.net
NIXLAND, LLC
444 W Ocean BLVD suite 800
Long Beach, Ca 90802
Tel: 562-624-2867
Fax: 562-612-1004
www.nixland.net

ISBN: 978-0-9884151-0-2 (trade paperback)
ISBN: 978-0-9884151-1-9 (ebook)

Library of Congress Control Number 2012951785

Printed in the United States of America
Book Design: Dotti Albertine

*Dedicated to
my fabulous grandsons
Timmy and Tommy Nix
and my wonderful family*

Tom Nix fought his way from the streets of San Pedro to create the biggest check cashing chain in Southern California. His company, Nix Check Cashing, became a valued and trusted institution among the underserved communities of South Central Los Angeles.

To build the business, Nix had to overcome armed robberies, cutthroat competition, the L.A. Riots, and an assassination threat by the Chicago Mob. His commitment to fairness and his tireless drive to succeed made Nix Check Cashing an integral part of the communities he served, and helped to transform the check cashing industry everywhere.

This book tells a great story through a series of true tales that are sometimes funny and sometimes gripping and shares the many lessons he learned along the way.

CONTENTS

ACKNOWLEDGMENTS

This book, and the adventures in it, would not have been possible without my wife Pam. She supported me 100 percent through the years, in the business and in life. Pam was my editor and chief advisor on this book, and an important part of the successes it describes.

I appreciate Linda Coleman-Willis for pointing me in the right direction with her "How To Write a Book" seminar "From Concept To Completion".

I'd also like to thank the people who read the early drafts of the book and offered their suggestions: Darline Gavin, my close friend and coworker for forty years; Denise Trapani, my old friend from San Pedro High School; Jim Taylor, a good friend I first met in the Sheriff's Department in 1976; Bob Padgett, my Kappa Alpha fraternity brother and current member of the USC Board of Trustees; my wonderful daughter-in-law Suzie Nix; and Evie

Compton, a new friend that I met through the Catalina Island Yacht Club.

I would also like to thank Michael Levin, Sara Stratton and the team at Business Ghost, Inc. for their amazing services including excellently editing the content of my draft, creating cover design, interior layout and design, and providing all of the other services necessary to publish the book. It has been a real pleasure working with them on this project.

I would also like to thank the Nix Check Cashing team: the workers who feel so much like an extended family, the investors who believed in our vision, the many businesspeople who provided Nix with services, and our loyal legions of customers, who made all of this possible.

I would like to recognize my mom and dad, Tom and Bella, who raised me well and were an integral part of the success of the business. Dad was my business partner, mentor, and best friend, and Mom was our enthusiastic cheerleader, who worked alongside us for many years when she was not working her regular job as a secretary in the facilities department at Northrop Aviation.

Finally, I would like to thank my two sons, Tom and Bill Nix, who worked in the family business for many years, and provided me with their valuable input. They are my real legacy.

Prologue

I am excited to tell you an amazing small business story, and I hope you will find it interesting, entertaining, and inspirational. It started with my father, Thomas E. Nix, who invested his life's savings of $1,200 in a business called Thomas Nix Bakery Distributor, which he and I evolved and grew over the years into an institution that became Nix Check Cashing.

When we sold Nix Check Cashing to Kinecta Federal Credit Union for $45 million in 2007, the business was an established and vital part of the economy and the lives of the people in South Central Los Angeles and the surrounding cities. It served approximately 400,000 customer transactions per month from fifty-five locations, an area that our top management team affectionately referred to as "Nixland."

This is the story of how we built Nix Check Cashing, and the lessons we learned along the way.

CHAPTER 1

Growing Up

No one is born a fighter. It's something you have to learn the hard way.

We moved to Ontario, California when I was six. I was a shy, little, baby-faced kid unaccustomed to being around other kids. My first day of school, my mom dressed me in white pants and a sweater. She thought I looked so cute. She walked me to school, and I was scared to death to leave her side. But she gave me a kiss, and said, "Get going," and walked away.

I only made it about a hundred feet before the roughneck boys laid into me. They argued over which one of them was going to get to beat up the new kid, and in the end, they just took turns. I had a fight with someone before school almost every day for weeks.

During that time, my dad taught me how to box and how to street fight. He'd been a roughneck kid himself, and then spent six years in the Navy, and it turned out he was a pretty great teacher. It wasn't long before I was winning many of my fights.

In the early 1950s, in my neighborhood, that was important.

I became good friends with a buck-toothed kid named Billy, and we would regularly defend ourselves together. One day, I told him I was better and tougher than he was, and we agreed to find out. We squared off and started boxing.

Before long, we were rolling around on the ground slugging each other, neither one of us willing to give up. Finally, a man came running across the field yelling for us to stop. I was glad to see him coming, because Billy was just as hardheaded as I was, and I was starting to worry he might actually win. The man pulled us apart and demanded to know what we were fighting about. When we told him we were best friends and were trying to see who was tougher, he burst out laughing. "It's a draw! Now shake hands." We both had bloody noses and were banged up pretty good. We shook hands, agreed it was a stupid idea, and gained a new respect for each other.

Later, when I was in second or third grade, I was playing in a field when four older boys approached me and said they were going to kick my ass. I wished Billy was with me, but even then, we would have been no match for these four big kids. I ran for home as fast as I could, with all four of them right behind me the whole way. It's amazing how fast you can run when you're in fear for your life. I made it to my house, and slammed the door behind me.

My dad was home. He opened the door and looked out without saying a word, and the four kids ran away. I was so relieved.

"What happened?" he asked. He listened calmly while I explained. But then he told me I did the wrong thing. "You are never to run. You always stand your ground no matter what." He told me that I should challenge them to fight me one at a time, and if they didn't, then even the odds by picking up a board or a stone and fighting to the end if necessary. Running was not an option.

He reached in his pocket and pulled out a silver dollar. "From now on, I will give you a silver dollar every time you stand your ground. But if you ever run again, I'll beat you a lot worse than those neighborhood kids."

My dad did not have a good childhood. He quit school in the eighth grade and went to work in a steel mill. After World War II broke out, he lied about his age and joined the Navy when he was sixteen. After the war, things were tough, and competition for jobs was fierce. Dad went to a construction site and told the supervisor that he would carry three times as much plaster and cement as any of the guys on the job, if they would just give him a chance, and when he proved it, they gave him the job. Dad was a very smart man with an incredible work ethic who was afraid of nothing, and he wanted the same from me.

Several days later, I was put to the test. The same four kids knocked at my door. My dad wasn't home, and my mom answered. She came to tell me that four boys had come over to fight with me. "You know what your dad said. Now get out there."

I couldn't believe my mom was making me fight those big kids. She went with me to the front door, and told them, "Tommy will fight you one at a time. Now who's first?" Of course the biggest kid stepped forward. He was a foot taller than me, with a much longer reach. After taking a few blows, I somehow managed to get him in a headlock on the ground and started punching him in the nose. I was frantic, and blood was splattering from his nose with each punch. I kept yelling, "Give up," but he refused. His friends were all cheering him on and encouraging him to break the headlock, but I had him in a death grip. Two of the other boys started to jump in the fight, and my mom pulled each of them off, yelling, "This will be a fair fight." I had whipped this kid, but he would not give up. In a quick maneuver, I changed positions and started banging his head into the concrete. My mom then said, "That's enough. This fight is over." She sent the bloodied kid back to his friends and said, "Who's next?" They all declined, and walked home. I got my silver dollar that night!

These early experiences changed my life forever. Growing up in that roughneck neighborhood of Ontario, and my dad's edict that quitting is never an option, were critical in making Nix Check Cashing a highly successful company. We never would have survived the many challenges we faced without the fighting spirit he taught me.

When I was in the fourth grade, we moved to an upper-middle-income neighborhood in San Pedro. My new grammar school, Crestwood Street School, was only a block away from my house on Upland Street. I was nervous about my first day at school, as anyone would be. Surprisingly, no one threatened me on the way into school, and class went well in the morning.

At recess, I went in the school yard and sat quietly on a bench by myself. Then a kid walked over to me and said something that I really didn't understand, but I jumped up and took a fighting stance. "Come on, asshole," I shouted. "I'll kick your ass!" I was surprised to see the kid turn and run away. I sat back down on the bench, and a few minutes later a teacher and the same kid approached me. She asked me why I threatened this boy, and I told her he threatened me first. "No, I didn't. I asked if you wanted to play tetherball."

I asked what tetherball was, and the teacher explained. I was embarrassed and apologized to the boy and the teacher. The teacher stood there while I played tetherball for the first time in my life. The boy was very nice to me, even though he won every game. He shook my hand when we were done. It was fun, and I realized that life was different now.

Growing up on Upland Street was a delight. I made many friends and fist-fighting was unheard of. I was getting good grades in school and having lots of fun. My world had changed dramatically. I graduated from Crestwood Street School and went to Dotson Junior High School the first year it opened. It was on the hill above Western Avenue and had a similarly good environment. Most of the kids came from upper-middle-income families and were easy to play with.

In junior high, the cool kids were smoking after school, and I was eager to be cool. My mom and dad each smoked three packs of cigarettes a day, and so did most parents in those days, but it was not okay for kids to do it, which made it even more thrilling. The very first day I had a cigarette, my dad smelled it on me and asked me about it. Lying was not an option in my house, so I fessed up. He had me sit at the kitchen table and smoke cigarettes one after another until I threw up. He then threw down a challenge: "Every kid can smoke, but only a handful of kids have the courage to stand up to the crowd and say no. If you really want to prove yourself, you'll be one of the courageous kids." I took his challenge, and never smoked again in my life.

I have a vivid memory from when I was pretty young, living in Fontana, California. I was friends with a boy named Tommy. We used to hide in the bushes near the train tracks at the rear of his property and wait for passing freight trains. If the train was going slow enough, we'd jump on the ladder to one of the cars and ride it a few hundred yards and jump off and walk back. We also looked for the hobos that frequented the railroad trains back in the 1950s. Sometimes, we would jump out of the bushes and throw rocks at them. Occasionally, one would jump off and chase us, but he'd always tire soon and head back to the train.

One time, though, a hobo chased us and did not tire out. He was yelling, "I'm going to kill you little son-of-a-bitches!" I kept thinking, "When is this guy going to quit?" but he just kept getting closer. We made it to Tommy's back door with only a few feet to spare. Tommy's mom was able to calm him down by promising to cook him a nice breakfast and to whip our ass until we couldn't sit down. The hobo sat in Tommy's kitchen for what seemed like an eternity, finishing his bacon and eggs and toast and coffee while we sat in the corner, watching. When he finished, he calmly spoke with us about the importance of being nice to everyone, no matter what that person's position in life. He seemed like a nice man, even though he was unshaven, smelly, and bedraggled-looking. We promised him that we would never throw rocks at anyone again, and we never did. The man politely thanked Tommy's mom, and walked off towards the train tracks.

This was a very important lesson in my life and one I never forgot. Then Tommy's mom whipped our ass until we couldn't sit down, as good neighbors would do in those days. This experience, and my dad's good example, made a profound impact on me: I was beginning to develop a strong character trait to always treat people right.

One day, I was walking to gym class when I saw a large ring of boys standing around something. I thought it must be a fight and hurried over to watch it. I was surprised to see one of the unpopular kids, a kid who was kind of an oaf and a little slow, standing in the middle of the circle, picking up pennies that some of the boys threw to the cement. It was called penny-pinching. Boys were laughing and calling the kid hurtful names. I was incensed. I thought, "This is just wrong to be mean to this poor kid." It didn't take long for me to step into the middle of the circle and say something to the crowd like, "If you want to pick on someone, pick on me." It was obvious that I was ready to fight for what I thought was right. The crowd dispersed, and I walked away with the kid. He told me he was afraid and thanked me for helping him. From that point on, I always made it a point to say hi to him. We were not friends, but we were friendly. Things got better for him with the other kids in school, and I felt good about that.

I've made it a point throughout my life to be friendly and respectful with everyone, regardless of his or her position in life. Somewhere I read a quote that says, "A great man shows his greatness by the way he treats little men," and I believe this is true. We need to fight for what is right.

My neighbor, Dennis Rouse, was in San Pedro High School, and played right guard on the football team. I was amazed at how physically he played the game. I wanted to be just like him when I went to high school. I began preparing by lifting weights in my garage two or three hours per day. I also ate as much as possible, to try and gain weight and grow bigger.

A few years later, when I started San Pedro High in September 1963, I weighed 160 pounds and not an ounce of fat. San Pedro was an old school built during the Depression. Most of the students came from blue-collar families who worked in the fishing industry, or on the docks as longshoremen. The town was very diverse, with many foreign-born first- and second-generation Americans: people of Yugoslavian, Italian, Greek, Mexican, African American, and all other kinds of heritage.

Football practice started immediately, and I made the junior varsity team, playing right guard. About midway through the season, I was transferred to the varsity team. After a couple of weeks, our coach, Bill Sexias, pulled me aside from lineman drills and told me he wanted me to try the fullback position. I told him I did not want to, because my goal was to play right guard. He said he didn't care what I wanted and to switch to fullback. But I told the coach I was not going to try the fullback position, because I only wanted to be a lineman. I'm sure a 15-year-old kid being openly insubordinate appalled him. He told me to report to his office after practice, and walked away in disgust.

In his office, he was stern, but not raging mad. He told me he was the coach, and I would do as I was told and play any position I was asked to play. When it was my turn to speak, I politely told him I understood, but the only position I was interested in playing was lineman. Coach was astonished and sat there in silence for a couple of minutes. He then told me that I had the ability to play a skill position, and that I would be a much better asset to him and the team as a fullback. He said there was no recognition for being a lineman, and anyway, I was not big enough to compete in that position. I told him I would eat constantly and lift weights and exercise, so by next year, I would be big enough to play. I had set my goal, and I told him that I would give him 110 percent until I was successful and he was proud of me.

He said, "Nix, you're going to play fullback, and if you refuse to do it, you're off the team."

I told him I understood and appreciated the opportunity to play for him, but I would have to quit the team.

He asked me to think about it overnight, then come to his office the next day before practice and give him my final decision.

That night, I told my dad about it. He called me a hardhead and said I owed my coach total support, but that the final decision was up to me. I tossed and turned all night, trying to decide what to do. I reported to coach at his office before practice, and told him that I was only interested in being a lineman. I accepted the fact that I would no longer play football at San Pedro High School. Coach said, "You are the most stubborn kid I've ever met. Now get in there and suit up for practice. You can be a lineman."

I was overjoyed. I became an excellent high school lineman. I played first-string offense and defense my junior and senior year, weighing 200 to 210 pounds. I was the co-captain the entire season of my senior year, made All-League, and played on the Los Angeles All-City All-Star team the summer after I graduated.

While I was in high school, I met a bunch of great guys and we formed a club, called The Essex. There were a couple dozen clubs in San Pedro during this time, and most of them had clubhouses in the rundown area of town below Pacific Avenue, a neighborhood that had been booming 'til most of the military pulled out of San Pedro and Long Beach during the '50s. It was a perfect place to have a clubhouse. Rents were cheap, there were plenty of bars and pool halls, and there wasn't any residential housing that would be disturbed by loud parties or street fights.

The Essex had a clubhouse on 6th Street, just south of Palos Verdes Street, above two businesses. One business was called Wonder Dress and Sportswear Shop and the other Linen Bazaar Infant and Children's Wear. The owner of Wonder Dress was an old Italian lady with gigantic boobs, and naturally, we called her Wonder Boobs, but she spoke broken English, so I don't think she caught on. She was always very friendly.

Our clubhouse had six rooms, each painted a different color. One room was large and had a pool table. Another of the other rooms had a secret entrance, making it a perfect place for underage kids to drink alcohol safe from police visits or inquisitive parents. This room was off-limits to everyone but club members.

By the time we were seventeen- and eighteen-years-old, we drank openly in the clubhouse, and threw raging parties. If the police came to break things up, we would open the giant metal doors that faced the rooftops of nearby businesses for a couple of blocks, and make our getaway.

My club members became my best friends. We were happy to have a family away from home as we began to earn our independence from our parents. It was also a fabulous place to party and bring girls. We had a special pride. It was a great feeling to be in the "in crowd," and afraid of nothing. It was also my first leadership role, and it set the stage for a lifelong commitment to whatever team I was a member. "It's all about the team" became my mindset.

We took risks, and we made good decisions and bad decisions. We were living life at a pace much faster than most high school kids. Our objectives were to drink, party, have fun, get lucky with the girls, and to stand our ground and fight anyone who looked at us in a hostile manner.

We had some conflicts with the other clubs, but luckily, this was an era when things were settled with fistfights. Knives and guns were not the order of the day, as they are today. Not all of our club members were fighters, but I had dozens of fights during this phase of my life. I enjoyed fighting and was good at it.

One of my most infamous fights occurred at one of our huge parties. A big, tough kid name Randy, who was a member of another local club called The Plaidsmen, was at the party with a girl named Tamara. They got into an argument and started yelling at each other. He said, "I'm going to slap the shit out of you, bitch," and started moving toward her. She broke a beer bottle on the stairway banister and began using the broken bottle as a weapon, threatening him, but this only made him angrier. "Now I'm going to kill you," he shouted. I told him to leave her alone, and he said, "Fuck you, Nix. Mind your own business."

I decided to make it my business. We fought our way down the stairway and onto the sidewalk. Everyone filed out of the party to watch. We began boxing, trading slugs to the face, and then started kicking each other as well. Somehow, Randy got me in a position with his arms around me, with me bent over, and he ran me toward a car that was parked in the middle of 6th Street. His intention was to ram my head through the front passenger door window. There was a man in the driver's seat, a woman in the passenger's seat, and two young children in the back, and the car couldn't move because of all the people gathered in the street.

Fortunately for me, the woman saw it coming, and rolled down her window. My entire upper body was jammed into their car. The family was astonished that I took the time to thank them for rolling down the window, and to apologize for the intrusion.

Then, I swung around and tackled Randy to the ground, and put him in my favorite "I'm going to beat you to a pulp" headlock. I now had the upper hand, and Randy was taking a beating, 'til he grabbed my balls and squeezed with all of his strength. It was an incredible pain. I poked him in the eye, putting my finger behind his eyeball, and shouted, "I will pull your fucking eyeball out of your head if you don't let go of my balls." He did, but immediately stuck his hand in my mouth and ripped my cheek back as hard as he could, yelling, "Take your finger out of my eye!" I pulled my finger out and rolled out of his grip.

The fight continued even after the police had arrived. They were waiting across the street for reinforcements, because the crowd had swelled to a couple hundred people who had stopped to watch the fight. A short time later, the police used a bullhorn to order everyone to disperse. Randy and I agreed to finish the fight at a later time, to avoid going to jail.

Many people told me that I got the best of Randy that night, that I really kicked his ass. I was exhausted. I went home to ice my wounds and some nasty bite marks. I was really banged up, but I got to tell my dad that I won the fight. He said, "My God, what does the other guy look like?" That was the longest and toughest fight I ever had. Randy and I never fought again.

Another amazing fistfight happened while I was in high school, on my first day at work as a box boy at Anchor Liquor. My best friend, a club member named Steve Papadakis, had an uncle, Tom Papadakis, who owned a chain of liquor stores in the South Bay area. He agreed to hire me even though the minimum working age in California was sixteen. My mom begged my dad not to let me work there since I would be working until 2 a.m. in Harbor City, a pretty rough part of town, but my dad said, "He's got to grow up sometime."

It was close to the end of my first shift, and things had gone pretty well, 'til two guys in their twenties came in and told the night manager they wanted a keg of beer. They didn't have enough money, but told the manager they were going to take the beer anyway. They made their way to the storeroom entrance.

The manager told them they couldn't go into the storeroom, and one of the guys hit him in the face with a quick right punch, knocking him back. I jumped to his defense and hit this guy with my hardest right, and he crumpled to the floor. The night manager hit the other guy, and the fight was on. My guy tried to get away but I continued beating him. The other guy ran out of the store, and the night manager locked the front glass door, and then ran to the phone behind the counter to call the police. The guy I was pounding reached up and grabbed an end rack of cigars and pulled it on top of me. Then he ran for the locked door, shaking it violently to get out.

When I untangled myself, I saw him kneeling at the door, and I thought, "I'm going to finish this guy off with a running punch to the head." Just as my fist was about to hit him, he moved his head, and my hand went crashing through the plate glass. The glass carved a chunk of flesh out of the side of my hand, still attached on one side by a small amount of skin. I pressed the flesh back into its proper place and held my hand against my chest to keep it there. I was shocked to see the guy I was fighting crash through the glass door, shattering nearly all of the glass, and cutting himself in the process. The manager rushed over and unlocked the door. I ran out to the parking lot and started fighting him with my left hand only, and I took a couple of blows to my face.

By this time, there was a crowd of about thirty people watching, but no one volunteered to help. A few moments later, the police arrived and arrested him. The other guy got away but was later arrested. I told the story and gave my personal information to the police, who were shocked to learn I was only fifteen years old. A few minutes later, an ambulance arrived and took me to Harbor General Hospital emergency room. I was told I could not receive medical treatment until my parents arrived to sign a release form. I called home and spoke with my mom. She started crying, saying she knew better than to let me work in that neighborhood, and gave the phone to my dad. He talked to the doctor and gave him permission, but the doctor insisted he come and sign the release form before giving me any treatment. My dad was infuriated.

The hospital sat me in a wheelchair and rolled me to a hallway to wait. I was sitting across the hall from a line of pregnant women who were also sitting in wheelchairs. Before long, a large pool of blood formed around my chair from the constant blood dripping. To my delight, the women across from me started screaming for someone to do something "before this poor boy dies." The hospital finally took me in and stitched me up. My hand was bandaged for weeks, but everything healed just fine, leaving me a nice battle scar to show off.

High school wasn't all parties and fistfights. I was also a member of the Knights at San Pedro High School. The Knights was a prestigious honor and service group. Members had to have good grades and be elected by the teachers. Coach Sexias inspired me to join and encouraged teachers to vote for me. The Knights were the smart kids and the student leaders, not the low-rider kids who cruised the strip or belonged to a club like The Essex. Being a member of the Knights helped set me apart, and focused me on graduating with good grades and the ability to get accepted at a major university. I took a lot of criticism from some of The Essex and other kids in town for being part of an honor group, but that was a price I was willing to pay for doing what I thought was right. I was able to stand apart from the crowd, when necessary, just like I did in junior high when I refused to smoke.

One day, in the tenth grade, I was kicked out of my Spanish class and sent to detention in the cafeteria. To this day, I don't think I deserved that treatment, but it worked out very well: I was sitting with my good friend, a club member named Joe Rusich, complaining about the detention, when I noticed a beautiful girl walking through the cafeteria on an assignment for one of her teachers. She had long blonde hair that hung well below her waist. She weighed about a hundred ten pounds, and had an outstanding shape.

I told Joe, "I am going to marry that girl." He told me her name was Pam Harvey.

That summer, 1964, I had a job at the local paper, *The News Pilot*, collecting money from subscribers who were delinquent on their account. I knocked on a door and was shocked when beautiful Pam Harvey answered. I thought, "My God, that's the girl I'm going to marry." After collecting the overdue bill from Pam's embarrassed mother, Pam asked me if I would give her a ride to summer school, and of course I did.

A couple months later, I started dating Pam. She was a

goody-two-shoes kid. She did not drink alcohol, and definitely wasn't going to give me anything but a kiss. In spite of this, or maybe because of it, I told her that I was going to marry her once I graduated from college. She thought I was crazy. She told me I was just a kid and had no idea about life. I said, "I'm going to marry you."

Our courtship did not go easily, however. Pam was fickle, and would break up with me about once a month. This gave us both an opportunity to date other people, but of course, as soon as I did, she would call me and ask to go steady again.

Finally, she gave me the advice I didn't know I needed. She told me my problem was that I was too nice. She didn't want a man she could wrap around her finger. She told me I needed to man up if I expected to marry her. This was a rude awakening, and a tall order to find the right balance. I thought, "Why does it have to be so complex? Why do we have to play games? What's wrong with me treating you nicely, you treating me nicely, and we live happily ever after?"

My dad gave me some advice to put things into perspective. He said, "Every woman tries to control and dominate her man, and the minute she does, she loses respect for him and has no use for him." Wow! I finally got it, and became less of a wimp in dealing with Pam, and it worked. Dad gave me good advice. I can honestly say I think he was right for most women. Men need to be loving, appreciative, understanding, communicative, caring, responsible, and all of the good things, but don't let your woman lose respect for you, or she will kick you to the curb. I ultimately accomplished my mission and married Pam a month after I graduated from college in 1970, and we have been happily married ever since, with just a few bumps in the road.

Toward the end of high school, I was recruited by the University of Southern California and promised a scholarship, 'til I broke my foot in my senior year at San Pedro High. I decided to join the USC Trojans as a walk-on in 1966, without a scholarship, and played on the freshman team coached by Craig Fertig. USC promised me a scholarship if I made the team. I was really motivated, because my dad had told me that he couldn't pay for my tuition past the first semester, since he'd lost his job and was starting a new business. He said if I didn't get a football scholarship, I would have to work in this new business for a low wage, and get student loans if I wanted to continue at USC.

In August 1966, I drove my 1959 lowered Chevy Impala, complete with tuck-and-roll-interior, four-bar hubcaps, blue and white teardrop knobs, and a fuzzy rear-view mirror warmer Pam made for me, from San Pedro to the University of Southern California. The campus is only about twenty miles from San Pedro, but it might as well have been a million: it was a different world. I was dressed in black bell-bottom Frisco jeans, a white T-shirt, Pendleton shirt, spit-polished black wingtip shoes, and hair slicked straight back with Tres Flores Palmade. This is what low-rider guys wore in San Pedro in those days, but I looked like I was from a different planet to the kids at USC. They were wearing penny loafers with no socks, corduroy pants, colorful shirts with sweaters draped around their necks, and short haircuts parted on one side. To say I had more than my share of butterflies in my stomach is an understatement.

I was lonesome for my way of life, where people dressed normally. In San Pedro, I had hundreds of friends, and a strong sense of confidence and security. I wanted to go home, but I knew that was out of the question. There was no running away from a challenge in the Nix family. I started dressing similarly to the other kids, and did my best to fit in.

I was very busy with studies, football, and trying to fit in. I did well on the freshman football team, and was one of only two freshmen players moved to practice with the varsity toward the end of the season. I was stoked. I was on my way to a scholarship.

But I had a rude awakening on my first day practicing with varsity. I lined up across from Ron Yary, who was about six-foot-six and 270 pounds. Yary was a great player and eventually became an NFL All-American Hall of Famer. My adrenaline was flowing, and I did my best to break through the offensive line. It was common for linemen to go at each other at 100 percent effort in practice. I got a break a few plays later, and laid a crushing tackle on the ball carrier. I was really proud of myself, until I realized a dead silence had fallen over the whole team. Coach John McKay led the practice from a tower about forty feet high, where he sat under an umbrella with a megaphone. It was his custom never to talk to the players directly. He would holler down over the megaphone to one of his assistant coaches, and tell them to tell the player not to do so and so, or to do such and such. Everyone heard the command, but the assistant coach would tell the player exactly what Coach McKay had said. I didn't like McKay's aloof, standoffish style of coaching, and I was about to like it even less.

I looked up and saw McKay throw down his megaphone and start scurrying down the ladder off his tower. I thought to myself, "This cannot be good." He came up to me in a rush, grabbed my facemask to pull me close to his face, and yelled, "You stupid fuck, don't you ever hit one of our fucking ball carriers like that again! Do you understand me?" I said, "Yes, sir, it will never happen again," and I meant it.

McKay then turned around to Yary and the other

linemen and said something to them. We all watched as McKay rushed up the ladder to the top of his tower. I knew I was in for trouble. He blew the whistle, and they ran the next play, which was apparently "Get Nix." I was crushed under the entire right side of the line. As I lay on the bottom of the stack, Ron Yary stepped on my right hand with all of his weight, and began twisting his foot as if he were putting out a cigarette. I saw my fingers and hand swell like filling a surgical glove with water. I thought my hand might be broken, but it turned out not to be. We finished practice and walked back into the locker room.

It was clear to me that I had made a mistake at practice that day. Linemen were supposed to toss it up with each other, but gentle tackles were all that was appropriate for the ball carrier. While I was in the shower, Yary came up to me and said, "I'm sorry I had to hurt you, but McKay told me to do it to teach you a lesson." I told him no hard feelings. I did not have any hard feelings for him, but I did for McKay. I felt it was no way to treat an eighteen-year-old kid who's obviously doing his best on his first day of practice. Just a little instruction would have done the trick. My hand healed, I finished out the season, and overall, I had one of the best experiences of my life. Playing football for the Trojans with all of the traditions, spirit, and high-level energy was an incredible experience.

We were going to the Rose Bowl that year, and Coach

Fertig told me I would be practicing over Christmas break with the varsity. I asked him if I could count on the scholarship I'd been promised, and he told me that they had decided to wait until spring, to compare me with the junior-college transfers before making a decision. I explained my financial circumstances, and said without a scholarship, I would have to quit the team and get a full-time job to pay for my tuition. He said he would check again and get back to me within a week, but he never did, so that semester, I stopped playing football with the Trojans, and I went to work full-time in our fledgling new business, Thomas Nix Bakery Distributor.

While at USC, I joined the Kappa Alpha fraternity. Being a KA was one of the best experiences of my life. I was part of an organization with rich traditions that was full of smart, aggressive guys. I was an enthusiastic part of the team. We had lots of activities and parties, but never lost sight of our main goal—to graduate from USC and have a successful life. It was the start of a lifelong motto: "Work hard, play hard, sleep when you're dead."

I had many growth experiences and forged lifelong friendships during college. USC and Kappa Alpha fraternity changed my life forever. It was a great education, and I graduated with a Bachelor of Science degree in four years. My college experience gave me the confidence to relate with people from high-income families and opened my eyes to new possibilities for myself. I had outgrown my low-rider days from San Pedro, but was still extremely proud of having grown up there. Pedro is a special place with a strong sense of community, and full of good, hard-working people. I feel very fortunate to be able to relate to people from all walks of life, thanks to the combination of growing up in San Pedro, USC, Kappa Alpha, and a career in small business ownership that help me grow in unimaginable ways.

CHAPTER 2

Our Business—Early Years

My dad was sales manager for Golden Krust Bakery for about fifteen years. Golden Krust had about three hundred home service bakery route drivers. Most of them owned their own trucks and were like a franchisee. In September of 1966, Golden Krust sold to Helms Bakery, which had about a thousand route drivers and was the largest home service bakery in Southern California.

As a result, my dad started Thomas Nix Bakery Distributor on September 13, 1966, and began distributing bakery products to the twenty-eight independently owned route drivers who did not want to go along with the Helms deal. He rented a five thousand square-foot building at 1985 E. Firestone Boulevard in South Central Los Angeles. He located there because it was cheap rent, close to the wholesale bakeries in downtown L.A., and in a low-income neighborhood that would support his plan for a day-old bakery thrift store.

We made our own fresh doughnuts each night, which we sold in the store and to the route drivers, along with other fresh-baked goods that were delivered nightly. It was common in those days for people to have the bread man and the milkman deliver to the home. It was a big treat for kids to run out and get a doughnut from the bread man or an ice cream from the ice cream man. Parents would even threaten their kids who were misbehaving to straighten up or they would not get an ice cream or a doughnut. Our bakery route drivers would pick up their fresh load of bread, pastries, doughnuts, and other baked goods each morning, and turn in their day-old products. We sold the day-old products in the bakery thrift store.

But things were changing by the mid-'60s. Housewives were going to work and many families were purchasing a second car. People were becoming accustomed to buying bread and milk at the supermarket after getting off work. This was the beginning of the end for the home service business. Over time, there were simply not enough people at home for the drivers to make a living.

We added more groceries to the store, and the drivers would buy them and stock them on their truck, in an effort to increase their average sale per customer and offset the fact that they had fewer customers. But this trend was unstoppable. Our route drivers, as well as Helms Bakery, went out of business within a few years. It was the end of the home service delivery business forever.

This was a very grim time. We were operating on a shoestring to begin with, and the loss of our drivers, one by one, seemed to spell the end of our business, too. One day, my dad was sitting in his office, gazing toward the front door in complete despair, when he noticed a small bird fly through the door and land a few feet inside. The bird looked around and hopped toward Dad, through the office door, around the desk, and up onto the toe of his shoe. Dad was sitting with his legs crossed, looking at the bird that was looking at him. Dad didn't move and neither did the bird. After a couple of minutes, the bird jumped off and flew away. Dad was flabbergasted. He called me in and excitedly told me the story. He said it was a sign from God that everything was going to work out okay. We were not religious and did not attend church, but we were spiritual, and this sign gave us the courage and tenacity to persevere with a new level of enthusiasm. We were going to make it!

Before long, the bakery thrift store had become the corner grocery market, and we changed the name to Mini Mart. We began using the name long before Arco coined the name for their gas stations. We became a full-service, mom-and-pop grocery store complete with a fresh meat department, produce, beer, and liquor. We were now exclusively in the retail grocery business.

We developed a three-pronged business strategy: sell bread cheap, cash checks for free, and give outstanding service. We sold bread at a very low price because we could still buy it cheap, as a result of our connections as a baker distributor. We sold six loaves of fresh white bread for a dollar, which was our cost. Occasionally, we would put it on sale as a "loss leader" and sell it ten for a dollar. People would come from miles around to buy bread; many people referred to us as the "bread store." This was a highly successful strategy that created tremendous foot traffic. People came for the bread, and most of the time bought other things, too.

We cashed checks for free. Many supermarkets cashed personal checks, and some payroll and government checks as well, but their policies were very restrictive, and they turned down a lot of people. Liquor stores would cash many of the hard-to-cash checks, but for a fee.

At our Mini Mart, we decided to make check cashing a point of difference, and took on a lot of risk for the sake of attracting customers. We bought a Polaroid photo identification system and made free photo ID cards for any of our customers who did not have a driver's license, so they could cash their check with us quickly and easily. This had never been done before. We put two bulletproof check-cashing windows on the back side of our office in the back of the store. On heavy check-cashing days, over a hundred people at a time would line up in our store to get their checks cashed for free. The line stretched down the stairs and most of the center aisle of the market, and sometimes out the front door. It was unbelievable!

We also gave fabulous service. We hired only warm, friendly people from the neighborhood, and my dad, brother, and I were overly friendly with everyone who shopped with us. We knew many of our regular customers by name. We greeted every customer while we stocked the shelves. It was a joy to shop at the Mini Mart.

The combination of cheap bread, free check cashing, and excellent customer service turned our little market into one of the highest volume per square-foot grocery stores in Southern California. We were featured in one of the grocery industry magazines, and this exposure encouraged numerous grocery store owners to call and visit our store to see how we could cash so many checks safely. I saw a business opportunity. We could sell our check-cashing system!

We became an agent for Polaroid Corporation, and a distributor for a device called the Photoscope. The Photoscope camera snapped a picture of the customer and the check they were presenting, and recorded it on one frame of film. This enabled us to prove encashment, if a check was returned for any reason. The Polaroid identification system produced a tamper-resistant photo ID card that enabled us to quickly identify our customer. We documented the practices we used to help us take the risk safely, so we could provide other retailers with a complete system.

We also used innovative approaches to identify a person who did not have a valid ID. We would have women with children bring in their child's birth certificate, so we could compare signatures. We would call a potential customer's supervisor at work and ask them to speak with their employee, to confirm the customer's identity. We would have existing customers co-sign a check for their friend or relative, thereby agreeing to pay us for the check if it was returned. These procedures helped us identify people who did not have legitimate identification, so we could make them a free photo ID card. This "window of opportunity philosophy" helped us measure the risk of cashing checks without calling the bank to verify funds and without calling the employer to verify issuance.

We created Thomas Nix Distributor (TND) Security Products Division to sell the equipment, film, plastics, and other supplies needed for our check-cashing system. Ultimately, we grew TND Security Products Division into a sizable part of our business. We opened satellite offices in San Diego, Sacramento, Burlingame near San Francisco, and opened our own film-processing lab. Over the years, thousands of markets, liquor stores, check-cashing companies, and other businesses purchased our equipment and supplies for creating identification for their customers and employees.

Our relationship with Polaroid created another business opportunity. We became a Polaroid-authorized Instant Service Company, which provided us with the training and support to provide instant photography services to malls and shopping centers. All of the major malls created elaborate Christmas sets as part of their holiday decorations, to entice parents to bring their children to the mall to get a picture with Santa Claus. Most of the malls put up a smaller set at Easter for pictures with the Easter Bunny. The malls would contract outside companies like ours, Nix Special Events, to provide the equipment and costumed personnel, and to sell photos to the public. The malls received a percentage of the sales revenue, and photo companies would compete to get a contract with the mall to provide these services.

Nix Special Events would start hiring and training personnel in October of each year so we were ready for the big opening day, which was always the day after Thanksgiving. Malls would schedule elaborate launch events, like hosting a magic show or flying Santa in by helicopter. Our employees worked for about thirty days until Christmas. Most of the elves were college girls, and retired men played Santa, some with their own real beards. The business was difficult because of all the employees it required, but it was lucrative for many years.

Among the many important lessons I learned while operating Nix Special Events, one was to take a measured risk (though, unfortunately, I would have to learn this same lesson a decade later, when I expanded Nix Check Cashing too rapidly). Polaroid offered us a fabulous opportunity to expand the number of malls we serviced, from twelve to fifty. They would sell us the necessary equipment at a drastically reduced price. All I needed to do was get the mall contracts, and then hire, train, and manage five times as many employees. I jumped at the opportunity.

It turned out to be a monumental undertaking. To make matters worse, it was a rainy season during an economic downturn. People stayed away from the malls in droves. We ended up losing a huge amount of money, and I could not pay my bills.

I took a deep swallow, and called each of my suppliers to tell them my predicament. I promised to pay each of them a small amount every month from the profits of my other businesses. I knew that any one of them could refuse the deal, and throw my entire business into bankruptcy.

We owed Polaroid Corporation the most money, because of the cost of film and the fifty instant photo systems I had purchased. I was relieved and inspired when they called back a week later and told me they would work with me on the film, and give me the Polaroid systems at no charge. They told me my up-front approach and my reputation for keeping my word convinced them. They said they'd had many customers in the past with credit problems, and I was the first to handle it the way I did. I was able to convince every single creditor to agree to my payment plan, and I paid them all off within about two years.

This lesson, along with many others, taught me the importance of reputation. I was committed to doing the right, fair, and honest thing. I was committed to always say what I mean and do what I say.

By the mid-1970s, the banking industry had developed a new approach to providing services to their business customers. They called it "account analysis." Each business account was analyzed to determine if the cost of the services provided by the bank outweighed the bank's earnings on that account. If it did, the business customers were to be charged for the additional costs. This created a new expense for companies that used a lot of services, like grocery stores and liquor stores that had made a practice of check cashing.

Overnight, our high-volume check-cashing business became a financial burden. We did not want to cash fewer checks, because it was one of the cornerstones of our success strategy. Our only option was to start charging our customers a fee. We held our breath, and added a flat twenty-five cents per check fee for the service.

To our delight, it did not hurt our volume. About a year later, we moved our fee to thirty-five cents with no loss of volume. The banking industry's increased fees had forced us to start charging our customers, and this created a possible business opportunity. Maybe we could charge enough for cashing checks that we could actually make money on this part of our business, instead of just offsetting costs.

We struggled with this notion for a long time, because it was a huge risk to take. If we raised our fees substantially and lost most of our check-cashing business, our grocery sales would suffer, and maybe even wreck our business. Our whole success was based on people traveling long distances to come to our store. Without the customer traffic created by check cashing and the purchasing power it created, we would have become just another low-volume, mom-and-pop grocer struggling to make ends meet.

We finally decided to take this risk, and held our breath again. We began charging our customers one percent of the face amount of the check as a fee. We initially lost about a quarter of our check-cashing volume, and we were petrified that it would get worse. Fortunately, within three or four months, we'd recaptured most of our volume, and now had a new profit center.

A few years later, I told my dad about my idea of opening a freestanding, drive-through check-cashing facility.

He thought I was crazy. We had never heard of anyone doing such a thing. There were a few, small, run-down, no-name check cashers, but most check cashing was done by banks, markets, and liquor stores as an adjunct to their normal business.

I was sure it would work. I talked to our accountant, and the two of us created a forecast. But Dad was in no mood for another hare-brained idea of mine. He warmed up to my freestanding check-cashing idea just enough to tell me, "Goddamn, son. Don't you ever give up?" Finally, he conceded. "Okay, we'll give it a try."

We had an employee, Darline Gavin, who had been with us for ten years. My dad had taken Darline under his wing and was mentoring her. Dad had a special gift for helping people grow and achieve personal success beyond their own expectations. He called it his "Bumblebee Philosophy." He said a bumblebee was aerodynamically incapable of flying because of its small wing size compared with its body mass, but it flapped its wings so hard that it overcame this obstacle 'til it was able to fly.

The Bumblebee Philosophy was an important part of the growth of Nix Check Cashing. We spent four decades looking for and hiring bumblebees. We sought out good, honest, hard-working people of character that we could invest in and thereby create an extremely loyal dedicated team of people. We didn't care about where they started.

We cared about where they were going, and we told them so. Most people are eternally grateful when you help them grow into a person who can do, be, and have more than they ever dreamed possible. This was one of the most important ingredients of our success. We had almost no employee turnover on our management team and very little with our full-time employees. We had extremely low internal pilferage even though we dealt with millions of dollars each day. Plus, our employees were motivated to do their very best. On top of that, we created tremendous goodwill in our community over the years by hiring thousands of young people as part-time tellers, helping them to put their initial building blocks in place and develop the self-confidence and self-esteem to move on and create a prosperous life.

Darline was definitely a bumblebee when Dad hired her to be our part-time bookkeeper in 1968. At the time, she was this little seventeen-year-old African-American girl, who was so introverted she couldn't look you in the eye. She never smiled. She was even afraid to answer the phone. Dad proclaimed that Darline would answer all phone calls when she was at work until she became comfortable with it. He saw something in her that I couldn't see at the time, and he was right: Darline became an integral part of our team and one of the cornerstones of our company's success.

We decided that Darline and my dad would run our first freestanding check-cashing location, while I managed the market, Thomas Nix Distributor Security Products Division, and Nix Special Events. Darline was an extremely valuable and trusted part of our team. We would definitely miss her at the market, but we wanted to give our new business every chance of success.

One day, in 1978, Dad told me he'd found the perfect location for our first check-cashing store. He said he had a gut feeling that it would be a homerun, but also that the site wasn't currently available. It was an old gas station on the corner of Figueroa and Imperial in Los Angeles that had been converted into an auto repair shop. He said he talked to the owner, but the man wasn't interested in renting.

I was convinced this would be a great location just because Dad said so. He seemed to have a sixth sense about things, and he felt so strongly about this particular spot. I decided to talk to the owner of the repair shop myself.

When I got there, the owner was working on a car in what used to be the lube bay of the gas station. He was kind of belligerent at first. "Your dad already talked to me about renting this place and I said no," he yelled. "This is my business, and you have a lot of nerve coming here and bothering me again." I apologized, but I had an idea for him to consider. "What if we're willing to pay you the same amount of rent that you earn here in profit each month? You could then retire or have the time to open another business."

I said, "To me, it doesn't make sense for you to work all month, with all of the risk and headaches of running your own business, just to make the same amount of money that we're willing to pay you for being our landlord." I could see in his eyes that he was beginning to see my point. I asked how much he earned each month, and he said about three thousand dollars. I offered him $3000 a month on a five-year lease, with three-year and five-year options, plus the option to buy the property at fair price.

He thought for what seemed to be an eternity of silence. I knew from my sales training and experience that the first person to speak in a situation like this loses. I kept my mouth shut. Finally, he looked in my eyes, and stuck his hand out, and said, "You have a deal." We shook on it, and agreed to prepare a lease and sign it as soon as possible. I knew he was a man of his word, and I think he knew the same about me. We signed the lease in record time.

Once again, I had taken a lot of risk for something I believed in, and it made my stomach turn over. We had paid at least three times the going rate for rent, for a minimum of five years.

Dad made it his personal project to get the old gas station ready to open. He was one of those fix-it kinds of guys. He spent six years in the Navy as a metalsmith and could take almost anything apart, fix it, and put it back together again. He did most of the work himself, and accomplished the task for a very small amount of money. He turned what had been the little office of the gas station into a bullet-resistant enclosure with two windows facing the service bay, and built a walk-up window facing the parking lot on the north side of the building, and a drive-through window facing the parking lot on the east side. He purchased bullet-resistant Diebold windows, the kind that were commonly used at banks in those days, and it made a statement.

We were ready to open. We were going to go about business in an honorable way, charge a reasonable price, and give outstanding service. This was in stark contrast to the few other check cashers in the area, who often had unscrupulous business practices. We were the proud owners of a new business, and we wanted our name on it. It seemed only natural for us to call it Nix Check Cashing.

Our new business started off with a bang, and just kept growing. We remodeled the building, placing a new teller line in the middle of the service bay, so the teller area was on one side of a wall of bulletproof glass and the customer lobby was on the other. We now had sixteen check-cashing windows, and we needed all of them on the busy days. In less than a year, we were cashing $1 million per week in checks. We charged one percent of the face amount of the check, giving us fee revenue of about $40,000 per month. The $3,000 rent wasn't a concern anymore.

In the grocery business, we never really knew how much money we were making until we'd counted our inventory to see how much had been stolen and how much had been thrown away because of damage or spoilage. This new business was so much easier. Our inventory was cash, and if we had a shortage, we knew about it the same day. We had no cost of goods, no inventory shrink, and no perishables.

It was a very profitable business, and we wanted to open more locations. In 1979, we sold the grocery store with the stipulation that they could not cash payroll or government checks, and opened our second Nix Check Cashing location across the parking lot from the store. This one was successful, too. Our business had changed dramatically, and we were excited about the future.

By 1982, we had opened a new location in Compton, and another in Inglewood. We were making money hand over fist. We had grown our little company to a team of about forty enthusiastic, warm, friendly people. Our strategy was clear, and we posted it on the employee bulletin board: "Our mission is to provide fast, friendly, customer service, at a fair and reasonable price, from locations that are clean, well-maintained, and professionally staffed with people who live right in the community."

We knew service was our key point of difference, so we trained and focused intently on providing the best customer service possible. We posted our Service Philosophy: "In order to be successful, we must sell our goods and services at a profit and still satisfy the customers. If we satisfy the customer but fail to get the profit, we will soon be out of business. If we get the profit but fail to satisfy the customer, we will soon be out of customers. The secret of doing both lies in the word SERVICE. Service means doing something so valuable for the customer that he is glad to pay a price which allows us to make a profit." We also asked the whole team to share in our business philosophy, "to go about business with a high level of integrity, a strong sense of fair play, compassion, and be an integral part of the communities we serve."

We knew that for any relationship to pass the test of time, it had to work for both parties. We didn't want the best deal; we wanted a fair deal. This approach to business set us apart from many of our competitors, and helped us create rewarding, lasting relationships with our employees, customers, vendors, business partners, and investors.

It also helped Nix Check Cashing grow.

CHAPTER 3

High Crime Rate

The vast majority of people living in low-income areas are good, honest, hard-working people who are striving to have a nice life. Unfortunately, they are held hostage by a handful of hoodlums and crooks, who prey on them and on the businesses in the area.

This criminal element creates major challenges for the businesses that operate in these neighborhoods. We were constantly on guard to keep our employees, customers, and assets safe.

Our own customers and the people living near our stores were loyal to us, and we had a great relationship with them. They would call and alert us if they heard of any criminal activity that would affect us or our customers.

But at the Mini Mart, our security problems were compounded because we were located across the street from a Los Angeles County Probation Department Office.

People who lived outside of our area would report to their probation officer, then walk across the street and shoplift from us.

Left unchecked, shoplifters would have put us out of business, so we almost always had someone watching for them. Most shoplifters were easy to spot: they would look around in a suspicious manner just before stuffing something in their clothing. Our objective was to arrest all shoplifters, except young kids (who would generally get a whipping after we notified their parents to come pick them up). We wanted everyone to know that they were taking a risk if they stole something from the Mini Mart.

To make a citizen's arrest that would stand up in court, we had to let the shoplifter leave the store without paying for the merchandise, and then detain them. Stopping and arresting them outside the store was tricky and dangerous. Sometimes they would comply, but many times, they would either run or resist, resulting in a footrace or fight.

My dad, brother Jim, and I all wore shoulder holsters with snub-nose .38 Smith & Wesson handguns underneath our powder-blue grocers' jackets. We also converted the wooden bread delivery room into a jail cell, to hold shoplifters until the sheriff arrived to take them to the real jail. We sent about ten shoplifters to jail each week. We were the Sheriff's Department's best customer.

One time, I ran after a shoplifter and caught him on

the Grape Street side of the market. He swung around with a knife, and I pulled my gun out of my shoulder holster so quickly that the bullet cylinder flipped open and dumped all six bullets to the sidewalk. I slammed the cylinder shut and told him to drop his knife. He said, "You don't have any bullets," and I told him, "There's one still in there, and I'm going to blow your fucking brains out with it if you don't drop the knife." He thought about it for what felt like twenty minutes but was probably twenty seconds, then dropped the knife and turned around and put his hands on the wall as I had instructed him to do. I reached down and picked up two bullets and quickly loaded them into my gun, then placed handcuffs on him. I grabbed the rest of the bullets and walked him inside the market to our wooden jail cell. It was just like the movie *Dirty Harry*, when Clint Eastwood says, "Make my day," but this was not a movie. It was another day working at the Mini Mart, trying to keep the thieves from stealing our business.

This was a harrowing time in my life. Every day was like going to battle. Our customers loved us and we loved them, but I never knew when I would be called into action to keep a crook from putting us out of business, and this was unsettling. We put a loudspeaker in the market, so the cashier could call a "code blue" if they thought we needed help. This would summon all male employees outside to assist. It was like the police calling for backup, and quite a sight to see all of our box boys and the butcher running to the rescue. Our customers knew what we were up against, and many times, they helped us when we needed it.

These were tough years from a security standpoint. I broke my right hand twice, got hit in the face with a hammer, knocking out most of a front tooth, and had a shooting that resulted in one of the criminals being seriously wounded and the other killed.

One day, a deputy sheriff who worked at nearby Firestone Station suggested that I sign up to become a reserve deputy sheriff. I had never heard of such a thing. He said that a reserve deputy sheriff was very similar to being a regular deputy sheriff, except part-time and volunteer. I would get the same Academy training, spread out over a twenty-six week period. If I successfully completed the Sheriff's Academy, I would become a sheriff, with twenty-four hour peace officer status, and work in uniform in a black-and-white patrol car. I admired the deputies at Firestone Station. They were tough, smart, capable, brave men who faced danger on every shift, for the sake of protecting the good people from the bad people. It was right up my alley.

I spent twenty-six Sundays and twenty-six Monday nights attending the Sheriff's Academy. I did not serve in the military, so being part of this paramilitary organization was exhilarating. The dropout rate was huge, but I was determined to make it, and did my very best. I graduated from the Academy number two in my class in 1976. I became a deputy sheriff, with all of the responsibilities and authority that came with the job. I earned $1 per year, plus $8 per month in expert shooting pay. I was part of a team that played a very important role in society.

I received fabulous training in the Academy, but I still had a lot to learn. Training in the streets was for real. We faced life-and-death situations and made a lot of decisions. I needed to do it right, make the right decision in shoot/don't shoot situations, write good reports, testify in court, and earn the respect of the guys I worked with.

We worked with training deputies, who were tough on new deputies, and certainly did not use any "win friends and influence people" skills. It was more like boot camp, with the drill sergeants barking orders in a demeaning way. I was determined to be the best I could be, and the best reserve deputy sheriff in the department. The department had about six thousand sworn personnel and six hundred reserve deputies at that time.

All Level One reserves, those with twenty-four hour peace officer status as defined by California law, were required to work two eight-hour shifts per month, attend one monthly reserve meeting, and complete periodic training exercises. I, however, worked one shift each week, and, in the beginning, I spent a lot of time on my own studying my new trade.

Reserve deputies would usually work their shift with a regular deputy. Within a few years, I was the lead deputy in my own two-man reserve car, which was unheard of at Firestone Station at the time. I also worked plainclothes with the detective bureau and gang detail. I eventually worked my way up to reserve lieutenant, and was asked to become captain, but turned it down because it required too much administrative work. I wanted to work in the field.

Working in the field was exciting. You never knew what kind of call you would get, when another deputy would put out a request for assistance, or when you would drive by a crime-in-progress and swing into action. It was a rough neighborhood, and the night shift was normally very busy. I would have my gun out of its holster ten to fifteen times per night, and there were usually several hot calls that involved a shooting, armed robbery, burglary, or dead body. It was fun! But it was also very challenging and dangerous. A bullet blew out a window and missed me by inches when we were in the process of investigating a "man with a gun" call. Most deputies suffered minor injuries from time to time, and several of the regular deputies I knew were shot, and a couple of them killed, in the line of duty. It was serious business.

It was also rewarding to be able to help people, and to catch someone who had needlessly hurt or robbed another person. The people who had been victimized were grateful. I had a unique relationship with many of the people who lived in the neighborhoods we patrolled, because they knew me from the Mini Mart and trusted me. They would often pull me aside and confide in me when they would not talk with the other deputies. I also had a friendly, open, customer-service type attitude even when I worked as a deputy. I saw no reason to treat people sternly unless they earned that kind of treatment. On the other hand, I was as tough as any deputy when the situation warranted it.

I experienced hundreds of what we called "drinking stories" during my time on the department. Here are a few of them.

My reserve partner and I were driving northbound on Central Avenue around 80th Street about 10 p.m., when we saw a black man in his twenties on the corner who was dressed just like the guy in the movie *Super Fly*. It was a popular movie at the time. We thought, "Oh brother," and decided to talk to this guy. He was wearing a brown Super Fly-type suit, a large brown hat with a white silk band, and two-tone brown and white platform shoes. He also had a long knife and sheath attached to his belt in plain view. He was completely out of place for the neighborhood. He seemed like a criminal type, up to no good, but this outlandish getup could've been some fantasy role-playing, because the criminals in our area didn't dress like that.

After getting his name and chatting with him for several minutes, I decided to give him some good advice. I said, "I don't know what you are doing here, but this is a dangerous place, and standing on this corner with that knife is likely to get you killed. Somebody might use your own knife to gut you like a fish. I suggest you move on." He said, "Thank you, officer, but I'll be fine." We got in our patrol car and drove away.

We handled a few calls. Family disturbance calls were common. They usually involved a couple that had been drinking, or at least the husband had been drinking, and a loud shouting match would ensue. Someone would call the police, and we would show up to try to calm things down. We would separate the two people, get their stories, and then try to inspire them to get along. We would usually tell them that if we had to come back, someone was going to jail. If the wife had been beaten and was willing to testify, we would arrest the husband.

We heard a homicide call broadcasted, and we responded to the scene. By the time we got there, another unit had already arrived, and the victim was covered with a sheet. I could see the two-tone brown and white platform shoes protruding from the bottom of the sheet, and said, "Oh shit, I know this guy." I gave his name to the sergeant in charge. He asked me how I knew who it was without looking at the body, and I said because of his shoes. We talked to him a couple of hours ago. I pulled back the sheet, and there he was, in his Super Fly outfit, with his stomach cut from one side to the other. His intestines were outside of his body lying on his groin and thighs. His knife was missing. It was an awful sight. I wondered if he was the victim of a drug deal gone bad, or if someone had killed him for sport. In any case, it was a sobering experience.

On a different day, I was working with a regular deputy. We received a radio call to assist another unit with a "violently insane person." The deputy on the radio advised us that he had been to this location before, and to use great caution. We arrived at the address, and the informant who'd called 911 met us at the front door. He said his brother was mentally disturbed and had been threatening him with a knife. The brother lived in the garage, which had been turned into living quarters, and we needed to enter the backyard through a locked gate that was located between the house and the garage.

Our intention was to assess the situation and, if necessary, bring him in for a seventy-two hour psychiatric evaluation. My partner directed me to take a position at the corner of the garage near a small window, while he and the two other assisting deputies walked down the long passageway between the garage and the house. We all had our weapons drawn. I carefully peeked in the window and saw the brother lying peacefully in bed. I looked back down the narrow passageway and saw the other three deputies standing one in front of the other, waiting for the informant to come out of the back of the house and unlock the gate. It did not look safe to have all the deputies standing in what could be a kill zone if all hell broke loose. I kept my eye on them, and finally saw the informant come out and start unlocking the gate.

Suddenly, the brother ran out from the side garage door with a large butcher knife, and started stabbing the informant in the back with a knife. My partner shot the man with the knife several times to save the informant's life. I swung around to the window ready to fire my weapon, if necessary, as I saw the violent man fall back onto his bed. He wasn't moving, and there was no need for me to do anything: he was dead. We called paramedics, and they rendered first aid to the informant. I rode with him to the hospital. He thanked me and the other deputies for saving his life. He went on and on about how grateful he was, and asked if he could hold my hand. I obliged. I comforted him the best I could. I was proud that we saved his life that day.

The week after this incident, I was working with a different regular deputy partner. We got another violently insane person call about midnight. When we arrived at the location, an older couple met us in the front yard. They said their son, who was in his thirties, had smoked some PCP and was going crazy in the house. PCP is a drug that can make people act unpredictably, and it gives them super strength without feeling any pain. The couple told us that he had broken nearly everything in the house and that he had a gun.

My partner and I called for backup, but we were advised that backup was not available and to handle the call on our own. We looked at each other with one of those "oh shit" looks. Inside, the suspect was trashing the house. We could hear glass shattering and other destructive noises. He was breaking everything he could. We saw him pick up the coffee table and smash it into the ground several times. We went to the front door, which was open, and called his name. He saw us and immediately took off and hid somewhere in the house.

We walked in with guns drawn and tried to make our way quietly. Every step we took was announced by the crunching of the broken glass scattered all over the floor. The prospect of having to shoot someone, getting shot myself, or shooting someone by mistake hit me like a ton of bricks. I was still shaken up over last week's shooting. For the first and only time in my ten years on the department, my knees started shaking violently. I could barely stand up. I asked my partner to give me a minute before we went any further with our search. He took one look at me and said, "Jesus Christ, Tom, pull it together." That's all I needed! It was gone. I had my courage back, and I was ready to do whatever was necessary.

We slowly searched each room until we got to the last

room, which was the back bedroom. We knew he must have been hiding in the closet. We called him by name and told him we didn't want to hurt him. We told him his parents loved him, and had asked us to help him. We were each standing on opposite sides of the room with our guns trained on the sliding closet doors. We told him to come out slowly with his hands over his head, and if he didn't we would kill him.

Finally, the door started sliding slowly open. I thought, "Oh fuck, I hope I don't have to kill this guy." He walked slowly out of the closet with his hands over his head, and completely naked. I looked down at his feet and saw two bloody stumps. His feet looked like shredded beef from walking around on the broken glass.

We placed him in handcuffs and took him to the station. After we booked him and he was transported for medical attention, my partner asked me what happened back there. I told him I didn't know, but that his comment to me snapped me out of it immediately. I thanked him and apologized. I asked him not to talk about it to the rest of the troops. I don't think he did, and we worked together many times after that incident. He was a good cop and I enjoyed working with him. After I left the department, I heard he was involved in a shooting. It is dangerous work!

I loved being a deputy sheriff. It was fun, challenging, dangerous, and gave me an opportunity to help people in need. I was part of a very special team of people, and had thousands of unique experiences that were only available to law enforcement. I considered becoming a regular deputy and making it my full-time career. After much fence sitting, I decided to stick with my business, and do the cop thing as a hobby. My wife Pam also said she would divorce me if I became a regular deputy, which went a long way in helping me make my decision.

Pam was already upset with my reserve police work, telling me she didn't sign up for this sort of thing. I normally worked the 4 p.m. to midnight or the 6 p.m. to 2 a.m. shift, and then I'd often have a few beers with the guys after I got off work. I would drag in about three or four in the morning, sleep for a few hours and go to my regular day job. In the beginning, I also had the arrogant, obstinate, super-aggressive, and intense, "my shit doesn't stink" swagger, which was common for new deputies. This made things even worse at home.

The Academy instructors advised new recruits to watch out for the three B's: Booze, Broads, and Bills. A lot of deputies didn't adhere to the advice. It was common for deputies to be big drinkers and to have marital problems. The job was extremely dangerous, from a physical as well as emotional standpoint, and had long, crazy work hours. On top of that, there were temptations from women who liked men in uniform and didn't care if they were married or not. A woman like this would be referred to as your "924." The department had dozens of codes to describe things and situations, so that people who were listening on scanners would not know exactly what we were communicating about. The actual definition of 924 was "station detail," and I didn't have one. However, being a reserve deputy was hard on my family, and it was difficult to justify all of the risk for one dollar per year.

It took ten years for logic to prevail. By 1987, my business had become so demanding that I just couldn't devote the necessary time to the Sheriff's Department, so I retired. I was able to keep my badge and retirement ID card, and to qualify for a concealed weapons permit, which was very important for our business.

My experience with the Sheriff's Department benefited our business in many ways throughout the years. It was common knowledge within the criminal community that the owner of Nix Check Cashing was a deputy sheriff, even after I retired, and I believe this helped keep our employees, customers, and assets safe. It may also have saved my family and me from being kidnapped for ransom, and certainly deterred any criminal extortion demands for protection money to do business in the neighborhood.

For several years after I retired, I missed the action, challenge, adventure, and adrenaline rush every time I would hear a police siren. Years later, in my fifties, I started periodically having a recurring dream, especially when I was stressed about something from work or home. In this dream, I would be in the Sheriff's Department, working patrol in full uniform, walking down a run-down, dark alley in South Central Los Angeles at night, gun drawn, looking for an armed and dangerous suspect. Suddenly, the suspect would jump out from behind some trashcans and start firing his handgun at me while running towards me. I would shoot him six times, hitting him in the chest each time, but he still kept coming closer and shooting at me. I would reload my gun and fire another six rounds but he kept coming and shooting. I knew that any second one of his bullets would strike and kill me. I was panic-stricken, and would wake up from my sleep, sopping wet with sweat. I never had these kinds of dreams when I was in the Department. I assume that by my fifties, I mellowed out, and the near-death experiences that once seemed so exciting had started to scare me. Thankfully, I no longer have that dream or any others that involve police work.

Early one evening at the Mini Mart, after I'd joined the Sheriff's Department, I started walking to my car to get some papers I needed at the market. I saw a brown station wagon idling at the stop sign with a Hispanic woman driving and two children inside. A black kid I knew from the neighborhood named Ricky, who was in his twenties, was jumping wildly up and down on the top of her car hood, denting it with each jump and yelling obscenities at the top of his lungs. He was obviously on PCP. The woman and children in the car were terrified.

When Ricky noticed me, he jumped off the car in my direction, like the Incredible Hulk. The car sped away and he started yelling, "I'm going to kill you, Tom, you fucking cop pig," and a string of other threats. I grabbed my gun from inside my blue grocer's coat, but did not pull it out, and yelled to Ricky that I would shoot him if he attacked me. He and everyone else in the neighborhood knew I was armed. Fortunately, his sister and another young man who were nearby rushed over and grabbed him, saying, "Tom's a good guy," and ushered him northbound on Grape Street towards his house.

I was relieved, especially because my hand was not quite healed from having broken it recently. I shook my head in disbelief and continued to my car to get the papers I needed. As I was walking back, three gunshots rang out. I ran to the corner of the building, feeling lucky that none of the bullets hit me. I was afraid Ricky might be running my way and would come around the corner any second to finish me off.

I pulled out my gun, which was painful with my injured hand. I took a two-handed grip and swung around the corner, expecting to have a shootout with Ricky. I was shocked to see Ricky lying on the sidewalk, with his sister bent over yelling, "He's been shot."

I rushed into the market and called the station, telling

them there had been a shooting behind the market. I ran to the office and put on the bulletproof vest I used while working patrol, and got a third handgun just in case I needed it.

By the time I got outside, the Cavalry had arrived, with lots of flashing red lights and sirens. A crowd was gathering, and the handling deputy, named Mike, told me to go into the market and wait for him.

About thirty minutes later, Mike, who was a guy I had worked with and knew very well, came in and asked me what happened. I told him the story exactly the way it happened. He then said, "When did you shoot him, and did he have a gun?" I was shocked! I told him I didn't shoot him. It happened just the way I said. He said, "Let me see your gun." I was offended, and said, "Fuck you, Mike. I'm not giving you my gun." He said, "That's up to you," and walked away in a huff. I took it personally and was pissed at him. I realized a short time later, when I calmed down, that it was a mistake not to give Mike my gun, because it made me look like I had something to hide. I didn't.

A couple hours later, the lieutenant on duty came to the store to talk with me. I told him exactly what happened, and he said, "Let me see your gun." I gladly pulled my .38 from my shoulder holster and gave it to him. He looked at it and said the victim was shot with a smaller-caliber gun. He asked if I had one. I said yes, and pulled my backup gun and gave it to him. He said, "Well, this gun hasn't been fired lately, but then again, you've had time to clean it." I asked him why I was a suspect in the shooting. He said, "We have a dozen eyewitnesses saying you shot him, and the victim made a declaration in the ambulance on the way to the hospital saying, 'Tom shot me.'" I said, "Oh shit. I had no idea." I thought to myself, no wonder Mike wanted to see my gun, and what an idiot I'd been to refuse to comply, making it look like I had something to hide.

I knew I was in deep trouble, and very disappointed that a dozen people from the neighborhood would lie about what happened. The lieutenant told me not to come to work patrol until further notice, because there was an investigation underway. I would be hearing from the department's Internal Investigation Bureau. I was completely innocent, but it would be my word against a dozen eyewitnesses. I was really worried.

A few days later, Mike stopped by the market to see me. My stomach was in knots. We sat down in the office, and he told me he had good news. They interviewed the victim's sister, and she told them the same story I'd told them, then added that Ricky was shot by someone in the brown station wagon he was jumping on earlier. She said the woman in the brown station wagon came back with a man in the car, and the man had shot Ricky as they drove by.

Mike said the initial facts all pointed to me. He said the

radio call came out that "Nix was involved in a shooting at the Mini Mart." The witnesses from the neighborhood saw me pointing my gun down the street towards where Ricky was lying, and they thought I had shot him.

Ricky was going to recover. He initially thought I'd shot him after he threatened to kill me, but he said he believed his sister's story, because he was out of it on drugs that night.

Mike said the investigation of my involvement was done. I thanked him for his good police work, and apologized for not giving him my gun when he had originally asked for it. He said, "Don't worry about it, it's over." We shook hands, and he told me he looked forward to sharing a beer with me soon.

I was ecstatic to have this behind me. A few days later, I saw Ricky's sister shopping in the market, and thanked her for coming forward with her statement. A couple of months later, Ricky stopped by the market and apologized to me for what had happened. I accepted his apology. We both agreed, "Shit happens in the neighborhood." They and their family remained our customers until we sold the market.

This experience taught me an important lesson about police work and life in general. Things aren't always what they seem to be, and can have very damaging consequences. It was easy for me to see how someone could spend years in prison and be completely innocent. I also understood how so many relationships go sideways, because people jump to conclusions after having false perceptions. It is easy to jump to conclusions and make a snap decision. I've made it a point to make sure I did my best to get the correct facts and to sleep on them overnight before taking action. This has been a very good practice and helped me handle situations in a better way hundreds of times over the years.

Our business needed a huge amount of money on hand to cash our customers' checks on high-volume days. At the Mini Mart and in the early years of Nix Check Cashing, we did not have enough capital or credit lines to order all of the cash we needed for a busy day, and whenever we began to run low on cash, I would drive to our bank with the checks we'd already cashed, deposit them, and bring back more cash. This was very dangerous, because it was no secret I was returning with cash. One time, someone cut the fuel line on my car while I was in the bank. They cut it only partway through, in hopes I would run out of gas on the way back, and be an easy target.

Another time, Pam and I drove up to Nix Check Cashing on Firestone just before opening. I got out of our van, as I did every morning, with my briefcase full of my Polaroid sales materials and other documents. A man at the bus stop walked over, asking for the time. He pulled out a gun and said, "We want the briefcase." Pam saw what was happening and quickly ducked down in the van. Another man ran over from the bus stop, grabbed my briefcase, and took off through the parking lot. The man with the gun told me not to move and began backing up slowly. When he got about sixty feet away, he quickly spun around and started running. I pulled my 380 OMC backup gun out of my wallet holster and fired six shots. Both suspects got away. I'm sure the thieves were shocked when they found no money in the briefcase. That was the last day I carried a briefcase or anything else into the location at opening time.

County checks used to arrive to welfare recipients on the first and fifteenth of each month. When the first or fifteenth fell on a Saturday, my dad and I would drive to Golden State Bank on Garfield Avenue in Downey and deposit Friday's checks, and pick up a huge amount of cash. Golden State Bank was one of the few banks open on Saturday in those days.

On a Friday prior to one of these cash pickups, I received a call from a man who identified himself as an LAPD homicide detective. He asked if I was the Tom Nix who was also a Reserve Deputy Sheriff, and if we were planning on picking up cash from Golden State Bank tomorrow. I said yes. He told me there was a strong likelihood that we would be killed the following day, and he wanted to meet with me immediately.

Two LAPD homicide detectives came over to the market

and told me that they had a tip from a reliable informant that a man had purchased a machine gun with the intent of killing us when we picked up the cash the next day at the bank. The police had the man under surveillance, and they could arrest him on the weapons charges as a minor offense, but it would be better to get him for the attempted robbery and murder. Otherwise, he would probably try it at a later time, when LAPD wasn't around. They wanted me to go ahead and pick up the cash, same as usual, so they could arrest the suspect in the midst of his crime. They said they had enough undercover police to make it safe, and a helicopter to follow the suspect along the way.

I agreed, but I told them that I needed a cop to go with me instead of my dad, in case something went wrong. We would need someone to run the business. They initially refused, telling me it was too dangerous. I said, "If you are not confident enough about your operation to go with me, then I'm not going to do it." They agreed to have someone take my Dad's place.

That night, I called the Fountain Valley Police Department near where I lived, and told the watch commander the situation. He agreed to open the firing range for me, and said they would handle any complaints they got from the neighbors. At about 10 p.m., I practiced shooting both of my pistols and the shotgun that we took on these big cash pickups. I cleaned my guns, and had a nice talk with Pam. I told her how much I loved her, and what a great mom she was to the kids. Pam was a beautiful young woman, and I told her she would have no problem replacing me if the worst happened. We also went over our finances and our life insurance policies. I had a restless night's sleep, but woke up ready for battle.

I met the LAPD homicide detectives and about fifteen plainclothes officers early Saturday morning in the parking lot of Security Pacific Bank at Broadway and Manchester. We went over the plan. There would be a few officers posing as pedestrians in the neighborhood around Golden State Bank and a couple more inside the bank. Others would be nearby ready to swoop in when they were called. They decided not to alert the bank, in case it was an inside job, but they did notify Downey Police.

I left the Mini Mart at our normal time with the homicide detective who agreed to take my dad's place. The surveillance team radioed that the suspects were in route to the bank, with the machine gun in the trunk. My adrenaline was rushing and so was my new sidekick's. I loved the rush, so I was excited, but a little nervous.

The suspects parked near the bank and watched as I went inside the lobby to get the cash. My partner remained in the car in front of the door, the same way Dad would have. The bank personnel were pretty shaken up. They told me that there were some suspicious people in the lobby, and to be careful. They said they had alerted Downey

Police and told them they thought they were about robbed, but the police had not yet arrived in spite of fact that they had called several times.

I knew the suspicious persons were LAPD undercover guys.

I got the cash, said to myself, "Here we go," and walked to my car, still waiting for me with its engine running. We started back to the Mini Mart, and got the call that the suspects were heading out of the area, back in the direction of their house. They obviously smelled a rat, and decided not to go through with it. I was very disappointed because I didn't want this threat hanging over my head every time I went to the bank to pick up cash. Something had spooked them. LAPD felt it may have been because Dad wasn't with me, because they had too many undercover people in the area, or someone working in the bank may have been in contact with the suspect and tipped them off that things didn't seem right.

I realized that, in all probability, my dad and I would have been killed that day, if LAPD had not gotten the tip and intervened. The problem was that the first and the fifteenth each fall on a Saturday or Sunday about three or four times per year. That meant Dad and I would be at risk each Saturday we picked up cash. I agreed to pick up the money together with my dad from that point on, and LAPD agreed to provide us a similar undercover operation.

times over the next few months, until

as no longer a credible threat.

dramatically for me as the business

:re able to hire our own security offi-

᠁᠁᠁h runs. We also didn't need to make

the trips as often, because we were better capitalized and
had a larger line of credit.

On one occasion, our armored van broke down on the
way to pick up cash at Community Bank in Huntington
Park. We called one of our other security officers, named
Jeff, to meet a second security officer at Community Bank,
and pick up the money without the use of the armored
car. Jeff was the first to arrive and sat in his own car in
the bank parking lot waiting for the other security officer
to arrive. Jeff was dressed in a white shirt and tie with
his gun, handcuffs and security badge, which looked very
much like a police badge, on his belt on his right hip.

Unbeknownst to Jeff, the bank was about to be robbed,
and the robbers wanted Jeff's car to use as a getaway car.
One of the robbers walked up to the driver's door. He
pulled a double-barrel shotgun out of his coat, pointed it
at Jeff, and ordered, "Get out of the car!"

Jeff figured the robber would shoot him as soon as he
saw the badge and gun on his right hip, so he grabbed the
end of the shotgun with his left hand and pushed it away
as he simultaneously drew his revolver with his right hand

and shot the robber one time in the stomach. The robber fell to the ground and Jeff handcuffed him.

The second robber fled on foot, but was apprehended by police a few minutes later as they were responding to the scene of the shooting. I arrived on the scene and waited for the police to finish their investigation, then took Jeff to dinner. He told me the whole story. When he was finished, I said, "Look at your tie." He was shocked to see a bullet hole through his tie, which had apparently gotten in the way when he shot the robber. I was proud of the way Jeff handled the situation, and gave him a nice cash bonus after we finished dinner.

In the late '80s, we decided to buy two large armored trucks to pick up and deliver all of the cash we needed, instead of hiring Brinks for the deliveries. We could lower costs and have the flexibility of creating our own delivery schedule, which was not always available through Brinks. Prior to that, we had to accept the delivery times that were convenient to Brinks. This meant that some of our stores would get late delivery, which required us to have more cash on hand from the night before. Our decision to buy our own trucks turned out to be an excellent decision when Brinks drivers went on strike, and again during the riots of 1992. We were able to safely operate our own armored trucks for many years.

However, we finally had a major robbery. One day,

our armored truck was making a cash delivery to the Nix Check Cashing located inside Food 4 Less in El Sereno. Eight men armed with automatic weapons had positioned themselves in the parking lot, waiting for our armored truck to arrive at its regularly scheduled time. It was the first of the month, so we had a huge amount of cash on the truck to deliver to the stores. We always added a third man to the armored truck crew on high-volume days, so we could have two "jumpers," the men who actually walk with the cash. As soon as the two jumpers got out of the armored truck, the suspects shot one of them and held a gun to the other's head, then took his weapon, while shooting numerous rounds at the bullet resistant windows of the truck's driver's compartment.

The driver's compartment was separated from the back of the truck where the money was located, and had gun ports that the driver could use to protect the jumper if he came under attack. But with this much gunfire to the windows of the truck, glass was flying everywhere inside the truck and some of the bulletproof glass began to shatter, allowing bullets to penetrate the driver's compartment. Our driver was unable to return fire and ducked down below the glass. The robbers got the keys to the back of the armored truck from the jumper lying wounded on the ground. They scooped out about half the money before our armored truck driver drove away at a high rate of speed.

We actually had very few problems when you consider

the number of locations we had over a forty-year period. But the constant threat required us to always be vigilant. We developed an excellent system to keep our cash and employees safe. We knew if the bad guys couldn't get any money, our employees would be safe, as long as they followed procedures. These procedures, which kept our people and our assets safe over the years, are still in place. We've had a number of close calls, but we only experienced three robberies in four decades that resulted in the loss of money, and only two that resulted in an injury to one of our employees. Sadly, in one of these, one of our assistant managers was shot and killed.

Our most amazing robbery occurred at our North Long Beach store on Atlantic and Artesia. It was about ten minutes before closing on a Friday night, and the manager had just finished waiting on the last customer in the lobby. He then went into his office and sat at his desk to begin the nightly closing procedures. The only other teller went down the teller line, emptying the small trash cans into a larger one, and walked into the back of the location to dump it.

Suddenly, a Dodge Ram pickup truck crashed through the plate glass windows at the front of the store, and on through the bullet resistant barrier that separated the lobby from the teller area into the manager's office, knocking him to the floor.

He knew it was a robbery, even though nothing like

this had ever happened in our company before. He rushed over to the safe room and began throwing bundles of cash into the floor safe, and spun the dial. The safe could not be opened until the next morning when the lockout timer expired.

The manager then started to run out the rear door of his office, but was stopped by two masked gunmen and ordered to get on the floor or be blown away. He quickly dropped to the floor as one gunman held a handgun to his head. The other gunmen scooped up the cash that had not been dropped into the safe and put it into a pillowcase.

They both ran out and jumped into the sliding side door of a van as it sped off. Fortunately, there was a Long Beach policeman in his black-and-white patrol car who turned on his red lights and siren to get the van to pull over. The van increased its speed in an effort to get away, and the cop went in pursuit with red lights and siren blaring.

It was a short pursuit, as the getaway driver lost control of the van and crashed into a liquor store. All three suspects fled in different directions. The police officer put out a radio broadcast and numerous police with the help of a helicopter cordoned off a large area. The police started their search and arrested one suspect, who was hiding in a plant nursery.

A short time later, the police received a suspicious person call from an informant, who said a man was hiding in their backyard. Police arrived to the residence, and then observed a man lying on his back with a handgun nearby and a pillowcase full of money, with some of it spilled out on the grass. The cops ordered the suspect at gunpoint to roll over and put his hands behind his head, but the suspect did not move or acknowledge the officers in any way.

The officers shot a Taser into the suspect with no visible response. They carefully approached the suspect, and discovered that he was dead. He had slipped and fallen in the process of climbing the backyard fence, and broke his neck.

We were able to get the location reopened in two days. We knew this crime would have been successful had the Long Beach police officer not been driving by at that precise moment. We knew the criminal element knew it, also. We had to do something to protect our people and our assets from future robberies of this nature. We knew the key to keeping our people safe was keeping our assets safe. We also knew that all of our careers and the tremendous needs we were filling in the community depended on our ability to prevent the criminals from robbing us out of business. We called it "Necessity, the Mother of Invention."

We decided to sink concrete-filled steel pipes about six inches in diameter into the floor of each of our lobbies at two-foot intervals. The pipes were sunk four feet into the ground and rose to a height of about four feet above the floor. A truck or car would have a difficult time driving through this barricade. We also discontinued the practice of counting the safe each night at closing, and had all locations do their safe counts at random times during the day. We made it harder to drive through our lobby in the future and reduced the reward as well. We never had another incident like this.

Necessity, the Mother of Invention, was always at work at Nix Check Cashing. We always felt there were lessons to learn from each challenge we encountered. We routinely assigned a focus group to document the lessons learned, and recommend changes to policies and procedures and the way we conducted our business. We were committed to running our business in the best way possible. We always asked ourselves, "What is the silver lining in this situation?" I've used this approach and attitude in every aspect of my personal life, as well, and reaped tremendous rewards in many ways.

CHAPTER 4

Cause and Effect

My life was going pretty well by 1976. I had a beautiful wife and two sons. Business was in good shape. I was working with Polaroid Corporation to provide Santa Claus photo services to malls, and had just been appointed to the Board of Directors of Spartan Grocers, a division of Certified Grocers, one of the largest wholesale food distributors in the country at the time. I'd joined the Sheriff's Department and was doing work that made me proud.

But I also had some serious personality problems that I needed to correct if I was going to achieve the happy, healthy, prosperous life I wanted. I was very intense, and had a terrible temper, and I suffered from huge emotional swings on a regular basis. The combination of these traits resulted in completely unacceptable behavior from time to time. I would act out and behave terribly. Then, when I calmed down, I'd own up to my bad behavior and apologize. Fortunately for me, most of my family and friends were forgiving, but I knew I had behaved like a real asshole, so there was no getting around it. I wound up filled with regret, guilt, and embarrassment. These temper tantrums were just not acceptable, and were damaging my life at work and at home, little by little.

I was also physically sick much of the time. I suffered from a peptic ulcer, which wasn't at all helped by my super-intense extremist's behavior, the dangerous situations I faced on a regular basis at the Mini Mart and working as a sheriff, the fact that I drank ten to fifteen cups of coffee each day, or the binge drinking I'd do on weekends. I felt terrible. I always got up when I needed to, but I was groggy and foggy-headed for a couple of hours each day. It was a struggle.

Around this same time, I was working at a Sheriff's Department recruiting booth at the L.A. County Fair with two female deputies I hadn't met before. We hit it off, and toward the end of our shift, one of them asked me if they could ask a personal question. "Sure," I said. "Ask me anything." They asked if I'd ever had thoughts of suicide. I said, "Of course. But I would never act on it." Then I asked them, "Doesn't everyone have suicidal thoughts from time to time?" They looked at each other and said, "No Tom, they don't. It's quite abnormal."

They went on to say, "We think you have a death wish,

and that's why you're volunteering to work as a sheriff at Firestone Station, when there are twenty other stations where you could work that are not nearly as dangerous. We think you are secretly hoping to get killed."

I was flabbergasted, and explained that was not true. I chose to work at the most dangerous sheriff station because I owned a business nearby. I enjoyed the challenge of near-death and dangerous situations, sure, but always felt I would prevail. And I certainly never intended to kill myself, even though it would occur to me as an option when I was extremely depressed or agitated. I really assumed that most people considered this option occasionally, and then blew it off as a crazy consideration.

But their questions disturbed me! I asked a few of my friends and they all agreed that my kind of thinking was not normal. I also knew that my very intense, aggressive, overly confident, adamant, sometimes abrasive, fuck-you-if-you-don't-like-it attitude was not normal.

I wanted to change these things, but I didn't know how to do it.

Mike Trapani and I had become best friends since we first met when he became an advisor to The Essex in 1964. I followed his footsteps into Kappa Alpha fraternity at USC. He was one of the groomsmen in my wedding, and I was his best man when he got married in 1975. We played racquetball at the San Pedro YMCA twice a week for a number of years, and then we started having break-fast together once each month. Mike was and is a highly successful insurance broker for Northwestern Mutual Life Insurance Company.

In the early days, he was regularly exposed to motiva-tional tapes and seminars at work, and he became a big fan. Every month, when we met for breakfast, he would drone on to me about how wonderful these tapes were and how positively they were affecting his life. He would always ask me to listen to one or two of them, to see what I thought. I always refused, because I felt I didn't need it, and I didn't have the time for this hocus-pocus stuff. My life was going great, so why rock the boat? I thought I must have all the motivation I needed just to be able to listen to Mike go on about the motivational tapes each month without telling him to shut the fuck up.

One morning at breakfast, Mike started in on how he wanted me to listen to a couple of these tapes. "Just try it," he said. I was planning to go on a camping trip to water-ski on the Colorado River that weekend, which was a five-hour drive. I decided to cut a deal with Mike. I told him I would listen to two tapes on the way to the river, if he agreed never to bring it up again. I had absolutely no interest in listening to these tapes, and Pam had even less. However, I thought it was a small price to pay to get him to stop talking about them.

He gave me *Think and Grow Rich* by Napoleon Hill and *The Magic of Believing* by Claude M. Bristol. I was hooked by the time I reached Parker, Arizona! This experience was a defining moment for me that changed my life forever.

Think and Grow Rich turned out to be the best single source of information I have ever been exposed to. I highly recommend reading or listening to the CDs of this book. It will change your life! It made me realize that there was so much about life that I needed to learn to be able to create a truly happy, healthy, prosperous life for my family and me.

One of the core principles I learned was that we live in a cause-and-effect world. There are natural laws that work whether we know about them or not, and whether we believe in them or not. A perfect example of this is the law of gravity. Gravity doesn't care if we believe in it or not. It just works.

There are also cause-and-effect relationships that exist in most areas of life. It was obvious to me that the more I learned about these natural laws and the other cause-and-effect relationships that affect me, the better my life would become.

I spent the next ten years listening to self-help and motivational tapes on the way to work. I became what's called a "tapeworm" (although now it would be a "CD worm," and that just doesn't have the same ring to it). I attended seminars a few times per year, and studied the teachings of the Church of Religious Science (now called the United Centers for Spiritual Living). I began practicing Transcendental Meditation, which provided tremendous benefit to me, and seemed to help me capitalize on the new knowledge I was gathering. During these years, I defined a new attitude and approach to living life, as well as new skill sets that dramatically changed my life experience for the better.

Listening to *Think and Grow Rich* started me on a crusade for information about how to live in a better way and be more successful. This process gave me the tools I needed to correct all of my issues and transform my life. I am now a very happy, positive, enthusiastic, healthy, fun-loving, prosperous person who wakes up easily and refreshed, without mood swings, temper tantrums, binge eating, binge drinking, or thoughts of suicide. I became a professional businessman and excellent public speaker. The people I've met and the many friends I've made over the last twenty years cannot imagine what I was like the first half of my adult life. I have mentioned to some of my current friends that I used to have a bad temper, and they look at me with shock and say, "I can't believe that."

I changed myself. I now have the ability to modify my behavior if I want to, and to achieve whatever goals I set for myself. The information I am going to share with you in this chapter allowed me to achieve happiness and success beyond my wildest imagination.

I took complete responsibility for everything in my life. I was no longer a victim. I could no longer blame my parents for the way they raised me, a businessman who took advantage of me, or anyone or anything else. My life was a result of the choices I made in the past, and my future life's experiences were going to depend on my future choices. I had the power to change most things in my life, and the power to change my attitude about those things that I couldn't change. I looked at life as a great adventure, good and bad. I looked for the silver lining in every situation. Experiences are our teacher. When things go right, we know how to do it next time, and when things go wrong, we know what not to do.

People who mistreat or take advantage of us are our teachers, just as much as those people we admire and respect are our teachers. I used to blame a person for mistreating me. I used to feel victimized. This attitude might be true, but it is not a productive attitude. Better to learn from the experience, and ask, "What do I need to do differently, now that this particular person has shown their true colors?" or "Maybe there is something I am doing that causes people to treat me this way." If you learn from the experience, you can change yourself.

I realized that our time on Earth is a journey and not

a destination. I grew up thinking, "I will be happy in the future, when things are more like I want or expect them to be." Once I took the "Life is a great adventure" attitude, I found there was happiness in every aspect of life, regardless of how challenging things were.

The most important natural law I learned was how the mind works, and how to harness it to create change in my life. The conscious mind is the conduit to the subconscious mind, and the subconscious mind works without judgment to create whatever is put into it. If we put good things into our mind, then we get good things back. We get whatever we think about it. This law is like the law of gravity. It works whether we know about it or not, and whether we believe it or not. It just works! A number of years ago I viewed a video called "The Secret," which I found on www.thesecret.tv, and which is a fabulous presentation on how the mind works.

Understanding this law gave me the power to change my life. I knew I was responsible for putting the proper things into my mind and minimizing improper things from my mind. If I could change my mind, I could change my life.

The challenge was how to put the correct thoughts into my conscious mind, so my subconscious mind would go to work producing them in my life.

I used visualization techniques and collected pictures

of my wants and desires, so I could view them on a regular basis. I stopped watching TV news right before bed, to eliminate that negativity. I was careful to think positive thoughts and to catch myself whenever I started thinking negative things. Creating a positive mental attitude was an incredibly powerful aspect in changing my life for the better.

I discovered the most powerful tool for programming my mind was the proper use of positive affirmations. I wrote sentences about whatever I wanted to experience in my life, as if those things already existed. Correctly written affirmations teach the mind a new way of understanding reality, and trigger the subconscious mind to begin creating the thing that you are affirming, so the affirmed thing actually becomes part of your life experience. Affirmations must state things as if they already exist, because this allows the subconscious to create this reality in the present, rather than postponing it until the future. Example: not "I *will be* calm, controlled, and professional," but "I *am* calm, controlled, and professional."

I wrote affirmations that carefully avoided using negative words. The subconscious mind doesn't pick up on words like "no" or "don't," so these negative words teach the mind to create the thing that you are trying to avoid. It is important to affirm what you want, instead of what you don't want. The subconscious mind gives you inspirations and intuition about what needs to be done in your life to make your affirmations a reality. You begin making different choices with different results.

During this period, I began saying the following basic affirmation to myself:

"I live in paradise, play in paradise, and have a charmed, fortunate, simple, blissful life, and a fantastic wife. And I am fantastic. I'm fun, friendly, likable, successful, rich, and the happiest, most fortunate man in the world. I have achieved all my important goals in life, and continue to experience higher and higher levels of joy, happiness, and laughter. I have fun. I'm excited about life, and have a strong sense of well-being. I am a positive, enthusiastic, healthy, handsome, honorable, fit, strong, studly man with class and style. I have an abundance of time, smile often, and am a calm, confident, capable, courteous, courageous, wise man with an outstanding perspective on life, who really enjoys living the great adventure."

Most of the things in this affirmation were not true when I first started saying it, but the vast majority of them have come true over the years.

I use affirmations to allow me to experience whatever I want in my life, big or small. Example: I have always been a mouth breather when I sleep at night, which is normally not a problem but causes me a sore throat if the air conditioning is running. I finally decided to do something about it and wrote this affirmation: "I sleep soundly for seven or eight hours each night with my mouth closed, breathe through my nose, and wake up refreshed." I say it as soon as I lie down each night and this lifelong bad habit was resolved in just three weeks. I have used affirmations successfully on dozens and dozens of things with tremendous success.

My use of affirmations gave me the tool to transform my life, and I continue to use them every day.

CHAPTER 5

Expanding Our Business

By 1983, I was a changed man, and equipped with the knowledge and personal power I gained from years of self-help, motivational tapes, and dozens of seminars. We had a fabulous small business that was extremely profitable and relatively easy to manage, with a loyal, honest, hardworking team of people who had fun working together. We owned four Nix Check Cashing stores, plus Thomas Nix Distributor Security Products Division and Nix Special Events.

My family life was terrific, and Pam and I were very happy. She had become a stay-at-home mom focused on our kids. Tom was nine and Bill was seven, and both heavily involved with youth sports, which required mom to cart them around constantly. We had moved out of San Pedro a few years earlier, and lived in a nice bedroom community called Fountain Valley in Orange County. We had a family meeting every Sunday night and discussed events of the week and what family activities or trips we should take. We'd also listen to motivational tapes for fifteen to twenty minutes that were designed for children. One of our favorites was Bob Moawad's *Unlocking Your Potential.* We'll still use one of the lines from his tape when the time is right: "No stinking thinking."

I had the kids give a two-minute oral report each week about the information they had been exposed to the prior week. I learned this technique from a Dale Carnegie course, to help make information relevant. The boys hated it, and it made them dread our weekly family meetings, but it was very effective. We started each family meeting the way Dale Carnegie does, by saying three times, "If you act enthusiastic, you'll be enthusiastic," each time louder than the time before. (We did the same thing at Nix Check Cashing to start our meetings.) We closed our family meetings by singing our family fight song, which is an adaption of the San Pedro High School fight song, which is an adaption of the Notre Dame fight song with the same tune:

Oh why fight for the family Nix,
You asked the questions, we'll give you the fix,
We are great and we are grand,
We are the best family in the land,

We have the power we have the might,
We have the spirit we have the fight,
We will win in life, you'll see the Nix family to victory.

Another family tradition was for me to say, "We are off," and the rest of the family to say, "Like a dirty shirt!" whenever our family drove somewhere in the car. My dad did this when I was a kid, and now my son Tom and daughter-in-law Suzie do it with their twin sons Tommy and Timmy. They also sing the family fight song, but have not followed my lead of having family meetings. I recently found a bunch of the tapes Tom and Bill used to have to listen to and wrapped them as a Christmas gift to Tom and Suzie. Everyone got a good laugh!

My life was fantastic, and my plan was to grow our business very slowly, and live the great adventure. But I saw a huge opportunity. Bank deregulation had created a vacuum for banking services in the low- to moderate-income communities. Banks no longer had "protected areas," and were now facing competition from the savings and loan industry and from credit unions, both of which were now able to offer checking accounts. Investment banks and brokers also provided their customers with checking accounts.

Banks needed to refocus on their bottom line, and realized they were actually losing money on their branches located in the low-income neighborhoods. The costs to operate these branches were higher than normal, because customers and employees of companies that banked there wanted to cash their checks, and banks did not charge for this service. There simply weren't enough savings or qualified borrowers to offset the bank's costs. As a result, banks closed most of their branches in low-income communities, and started focusing on high net-worth individuals and commercial accounts. Check-cashing companies were rushing in to fill the void left by the banks. A new industry was being formed.

We needed to expand our business to capitalize on this opportunity, but we were unable to get financing from the bank. I decided to form a limited partnership for $240,000 to fund the opening of one new branch and the cash inventory needed to operate it.

Dad was beside himself. He thought I was crazy, and adamantly refused to go along with my idea. I shared my vision of building a large company that filled important needs in a fair manner, with happy, productive employees and happy investors. He shared his vision of maintaining our small business, which was extremely profitable, with very few headaches and no investor's ass to kiss.

We each owned 50 percent of the business, and needed a consensus on any major decision. This required excellent negotiation and salesmanship skills, but the process almost always resulted in making better business decisions.

I used a consensus form of management even after Dad died. I would encourage my executive team to sell me on their ideas, and most of the time, we would go around and around until all facets of the decision were evaluated. Occasionally, no matter how hard we tried, we could not reach consensus, and I would tell everyone we were going to do it my way. But I tried to avoid this, because it short-circuited the process and disrupted the team.

This was certainly the case with Dad and me regarding growing our small business. He just could not understand why I wanted to sign up for all of the risk and the grief when everything was just perfect as it was. Pam was also highly upset and in tears over my grandiose plans. I would not listen to reason. I had a burning desire to grow the company and cash in on the rewards the banking industry was creating. I am tenacious and would not give up on my dream.

Finally, Dad said to me, "I think you are a fucking idiot for wanting to wreck what we have, but I'm pushing sixty years old and you're a young man, so if this is what you want, I will go along with it." I rejoiced and thanked him enthusiastically. I had no idea how many times over the next twenty years I would wish I had listened to Dad and Pam.

I wrote a ten-page overview of the investment that I planned to use to raise capital. I was excited to show my good friend Tom Barrack my document, and share my enthusiasm for taking full advantage of the opportunity to grow our business. Tom was an extremely successful and experienced businessman at the time, and would later form Colony Capital, one of the world's leading real estate investment firms. We spent the weekend with him and his wife Christie at their ranch in Santa Inez. It was a beautiful place and we had a fabulous time. One of the highlights of our visit was checking out his new barn that was used for breeding his stud racehorses. Shortly afterwards, I got the opportunity to tell Tom about my vision.

He had a ton of questions, and it was clear to me that I had not considered many things. One of the easier questions was, "How difficult is it to run the business?" I replied, "It's as simple as running your barn operation." He laughed and said, "I hope so."

Then I gave him my ten-page document. He told me in no uncertain terms that I could not use that document to raise capital. "Why not?" I asked. He said, "Come with me," and we walked from his ranch house to his office in a separate building. He pulled out a half a dozen private offering memorandums. I'd never seen one. Each document was over a hundred pages, and he flipped through them, showing me different aspects of each document. It was an eye-opening experience, and I quickly realized how naïve I was. Creating a private offering memorandum was an involved process that required an attorney experienced in this area. There were many rules, regulations, and legal risks involved in raising private capital without a broker. I was grateful that Tom took the time to point me in the right direction.

A couple months later, I had an offering memorandum for Nix Check Cashing # 5 Limited Partnership. The legal expense was about $20,000, which was a huge amount of money for our little company. We would get our money back, provided I could convince enough people to invest a total of $240,000. The minimum investment was $18,000. This was going to be a new business, separate from the rest of our company, but I could showcase our existing business because we were going to do more of the same.

I began calling all of my friends, Kappa Alpha fraternity brothers I met at USC, relatives, and business contacts. Fortunately, I had sales experience from the days of cold calling markets and liquor stores to sell Polaroid and Photoscope cameras that were part of my check-cashing system. Sales and cold calls require a thick skin because of all of the rejection, and selling to retailers in the inner city was especially difficult because they could be incredibly abrupt and offensive. I never took the first "No" for an answer, though this sometimes got me in trouble. One time, a liquor store owner got so perturbed with me that he pulled a gun from underneath the counter and pointed it at me, saying, "Get the fuck out of my store." I calmly said, "Well, I guess you are really not interested." I thanked him for his time and walked out of the store.

I was not always that thick-skinned. In the early days of outside sales, I got sick from a nervous stomach every Sunday night. I was so sick by Monday morning that I would usually throw up. But by the end of the day Monday, I was in the groove, and stayed that way the entire week, 'til the following Sunday night, and the process would start all over. I even went to my dad and told him I was not cut out for this kind of work, and he said, "Oh bullshit, you'll get through it and be a better man for it." It was a frustrating reminder that quitting was not allowed. Of course, Dad was right, and soon, I really enjoyed selling and was good at it.

It was easy for me to call my friends, fraternity brothers, family, and business contacts and talk about my vision. I felt absolutely positive that this would be the best investment they could make. It was going to be a homerun. The objective of my call was to sell a tour of our business. If I could sell the tour, then I could sign up an investor 80 percent of the time. I was able to raise almost $1 million in a few months, and funded Nix Check Cashing # 5 Limited Partnership, as well as # 6, # 7, and # 8.

Over the next three years, we funded eleven more branches and brought in dozens of other investors. We raised a total of $4.6 million in equity capital that allowed us to expand the Nix Check Cashing chain to nineteen stores by 1987. I will always be grateful to my friends and relatives who had the faith, trust, and confidence to risk their money in my dream and me.

We had a fantastic investor group. Everyone was excited to be part of something special. We were creating a company like no other in the check-cashing business. We were a company that cared about its employees, customers, community, and investors. We had a quarterly investor letter, paid quarterly dividends, and had an annual investor dinner meeting with live entertainment that most of our investors and their wives would attend. It was a gala affair. Our first and last investor dinner was held at Papadakis Taverna in San Pedro, which was owned by my very good friend and large investor, John Papadakis.

We had a grand celebration whenever we opened a Nix location. We picked up each investor in a limousine at their home and brought them to the main office for light lunch and overview of the branch they had invested in. We then created a motorcade of limos complete with motorcycle escort to stop traffic at the stoplights similar to a funeral so we could all arrive at the location together. It was quite a sight to see eight or ten limos traveling through the inner city in a motorcade. People assumed we were dignitaries with our plainclothes security officers who looked like

Secret Service Agents. They were dignitaries to me. They were the people who provided the seed money to change the way financial services were delivered to low-income communities across the country, the people who elevated check cashers to a respected part of the business community.

Much of the check-cashing industry at that time was despicable. Their locations were rundown, service was terrible, they didn't hire from the community, had no brand name on the storefront, charged exorbitant fees, took advantage of people, and played no part in supporting worthwhile community causes. They were the exact opposite of Nix Check Cashing, and an embarrassment to me personally.

We needed an industry trade group that would elevate the standards of check cashing, and support reasonable legislation. I was one of the founders of the California Check Cashers Association in 1983, and its president for many years. This organization later changed its name to the Community Financial Service Providers Association. In 1987, I was one of the founders of the National Check Cashers Association and its vice president until 1992. This organization later changed its name to the Financial Service Centers of America. In 1990 and 1991, I spearheaded consumer protection legislation in California while I was president of the California Check Cashers

Association. This law required check cashers to register with the Department of Corporations, post their fees in a prominent and conspicuous manner, give a receipt with each transaction, and charge no more than 3 percent when cashing in a government or payroll check, or 3.5 percent if the customer did not have legitimate identification. Overnight, we eliminated the price gougers and moved one step closer to creating a respectable industry.

Nix Check Cashing had a great relationship with the communities we served. We always believed that we were not just a business located in the community, but that we were a part of the community, affected by all the good and bad things that happened there. Because of this philosophy, we were embraced by the people in the community. Our customers trusted us.

We often had customers who would cash a large check, convert it into a money order, and then ask us to store it for them in our safe—using us as a kind of savings account. We would encourage these customers to deposit their money in a bank instead, but banks would often refuse these customers. So we became their bank.

We would also receive calls from our customers, to inform us about seedy characters loitering in the area. In turn, we would alert the community to scams and con artists. In one such scam, senior citizens began receiving a notification they'd won $3,000 in a contest, and all they had to do to collect was submit a payment of $1,000 to the con artist. Nix Check Cashing did an investigation into the con and we were able to shut it down.

Our company always supported worthwhile community causes, and as we grew, we were able to create a scholarship program. The Nix Check Cashing Scholarship Program was developed to support the needs of young people in our community who graduated from high school and did not have the finances to go to college or trade school. We worked with local schools and churches to find candidates for the scholarships. We would issue $1000 scholarships for students attending a four-year college or university and $300 to $500 scholarships for students attending junior college or trade school. Each year, we would have hundreds of applicants. The need was so great in the communities we served that I decided to ask our vendors to participate in this program. MoneyGram Inc., our wire transfer and money order company, agreed to match our dollar amount, and we were able to double the amount of scholarships that were awarded.

Nix Check Cashing was also responsible for an annual holiday food drive, which became our signature community support program. For three weeks, beginning each November, we would ask our customers to make a small donation to our annual food drive. Most people would contribute spare change, but some would make a larger donation. We collected about $75,000, which is an astonishing amount of coins. We also asked the corporations we did business with to make a donation. We coordinated with about thirty community organizations to identify needy families, and each branch would select three families from their own customer base. Nix Check Cashing contributed all of the labor, point of sale materials and other expenses, plus advertised it on the radio, so that 100 percent of the donated money went to the needy families. Each family would receive a bag of groceries and a $75 gift certificate from Ralph's/Food 4 Less, entitling them to a free turkey.

On the Sunday before Thanksgiving, about a hundred of our employees and their families would volunteer their time to hand out the groceries and certificates to over twelve hundred families. One year, at one of our distributions, a customer approached me in tears. She had recently lost her job, and was the sole provider for her five children. She did not know how she was going to provide Thanksgiving dinner for her family, and the certificate and groceries would not only help on Thanksgiving but would allow her to purchase food that would last for at least two weeks. The next year she was back to work and on her feet. She came into Nix, made a $100 donation to the food drive and said she wanted to be a blessing to someone else just as she had been blessed the year before.

(I am pleased that Kinecta Federal Credit Union/Nix

Check Cashing is continuing this tradition, which was started over thirty-five years ago.)

We also had a summer youth employment program where we would hire dozens of young people to paint our locations and do odd jobs. Many of them would go on to become part-time tellers. Our training program helped them develop job skills and the self-confidence to build a career for themselves either at Nix or move on to some other line of work. We trained thousands of young people over the years. We worked with the Shell Youth Services Academy, which was a program designed by Shell Oil to provide job-training skills and provide hands-on work experience to young people. We mentored over a hundred youngsters with Shell. I was proud to be their keynote speaker at graduation one year.

We were dedicated to our employees and had a family feeling in our company. We hired almost exclusively from the communities we served, and employed approximately four hundred and fifty people at the time we sold the company. All of our branch personnel had a quarterly incentive program, and all employees participated in our annual profit-sharing program. We believed in a decentralized form of management, and made every effort to create an ownership mindset within our team. Our store managers had the authority to make most decisions on their own and were held accountable for them, with a quarterly bonus program that measured ten key result areas such as sales, return checks, labor expense, shortages, and customer service. Our incentive program was designed so that any results that benefited the company would also benefit the employee, and vice versa.

We felt it was the job of top and middle management to give our employees the tools they needed to be successful. We tried to measure all of our policies and procedures by common sense and our business philosophy—"Go about business with a high level of integrity, a strong sense of fair play, compassion, and being an integral part of the communities we served."

Each of our district managers and branch managers had a monthly meeting with their employees, and top management had a quarterly, company-wide Manager's meeting. Each year, the managers who had earned an excellent review would go on a three-day trip to Las Vegas, with their guests and with spending money. It was fun, recognized our top performers, created team spirit, and was a fabulous motivator. Managers would say to each other, "Did you make the bus this year?" We also treated all of our employees to an expensive Christmas party at a nice restaurant or hotel and a pizza bowling night each year. These were great team-building opportunities and our team really enjoyed them.

We had an excited, motivated, inspired team of people,

who were proud to provide fast, friendly, courteous service at a fair price to hundreds of thousands of customers each month. This gave us a huge competitive edge over our competition, and helped us create the highest volume per store check-cashing chain in the nation. Sam Walton, founder of Wal-Mart, said, "If you want the people in the stores to take care of our customers, we've got to take care of the people in the stores." I believe this is one of the cornerstones of Wal-Mart's success, and in my experience, it's a rare attitude in large retail companies.

Another key ingredient of our high-volume stores was our well-known brand name. This was a huge advantage over competition because we could advertise on the radio, bus benches, and billboards, and create top-of-mind awareness. People were more likely to choose Nix when they moved, got a different job, or became dissatisfied with their current provider. New customers to the industry were also more likely to choose Nix. Our radio advertising, community outreach programs, and word-of-mouth advertising drove customers to our doors. We were the McDonald's of the check-cashing industry. Customers could count on consistently excellent service, the same fair pricing at all locations, a clean, well-maintained facility, easy access, and ample parking.

Our customers were also able to cash their checks using their Nix Check Cashing ID card or their driver's license at any Nix location, which made it more convenient and valuable to be a Nix customer. The Nix Check Cashing card became so commonplace in South Central Los Angeles and the surrounding communities that police routinely accepted it as valid identification.

Volume is the key to producing profits in the check-cashing business. Most of the expenses are relatively fixed, and there is no cost of goods sold as there is in a retail business. Once the revenue was high enough to cover the rent, insurance, maintenance, and labor, about 70 percent of the additional revenue became profit. The key variable expenses were returned checks, bank charges, shortages, and additional labor to adequately serve more customers.

This fixed-cost nature of the business also created significant losses while building up a new store or operating a low-volume store.

Our brand name also created a serious challenge for us that our competition didn't face: bad check artists could get our free pocket calendar that listed all of our locations and run our chain, cashing bad checks at one location after another for a few days, before the first check would return and reveal the bad checks.

This forced us to create a point-of-sale computer system that communicated information in a timely manner between branches. We needed all branches in our chain to be aware when a customer presented a check after already cashing one at a different branch the same day. Normal customers didn't behave this way, so it almost always meant a bad check.

There were no software programs designed for the check-cashing industry in the mid-'80s, so we had to build one from scratch. Darline and I developed the system we wanted on paper, then created a small focus group of employees to help us refine it. We spent months investigating major mainframe companies like IBM and Hewlett-Packard. They would bring in a half a dozen people to our office to make presentations, offering to develop our computer system. They were all cost prohibitive for our little company.

We decided to use PCs for our hardware and a small software company to write the software. This was in the infancy stage of the private computer industry, so we were on the cutting edge. It was a monumental undertaking to develop, test, install, and debug the system and to train our employees in its use. We also had to enter every single customer in the computer, at a time when consumers were unaccustomed to dealing with computers. It was a grueling experience, and it took us about three years from inception 'til we had a smooth running system that our employees and customers enjoyed. But it was worth it! It gave us all of the safeguards we needed to protect ourselves from criminals.

We had all the elements in place to build a huge company. We could dominate the competition with our new computer platform, brand name, and the experience, expertise, systems, procedures, and ability to deliver outstanding customer service with a highly motivated team of people.

We were getting noticed. We had articles in many local newspapers, magazines, and TV news. We were featured in a skit on MADtv and were in the lyrics of a couple of rap songs. The Beastie Boys mentioned us in their hit song, "High Plains Drifter:"

I said I'm charming and dashing I'm rental car bashing Phony paper passing at Nix Check Cashing.

In 1989, we began looking for ways to capitalize our business without forming more limited partnerships. Our investor group was pretty well tapped out; plus, it took a huge amount of time and effort to raise capital one person at a time. On top of that, we needed to expand more rapidly, because the marketplace was becoming highly competitive.

We considered using a small brokerage firm that could create and sell a limited partnership for ten branches. We also contacted three main suppliers to the industry about providing us growth capital: American Express, Travelers Express, and Western Union.

American Express was the leading provider of money orders in the country. They were interested in investing $10 million in our company, but wanted to keep it confidential. They were concerned about a backlash from the industry. We sold Travelers Express money orders, and, at the time, this was American Express's main competitor, so they saw an advantage in getting our account. We sold a very large volume of money orders, and they could point to us as a good example of why other companies should switch from Travelers Express to American Express money orders. We could be their flagship account.

Travelers Express visited us several times and was interested in possibly investing with us, but never made a proposal.

Western Union was interested in creating a joint venture company. They wanted to build a nationwide chain of check-cashing stores, which would give them a captive distribution network for their money transfer and other products. They were excited about our business model, computer platform, and management ability. In June 1990, they agreed to pay us $100,000 per month in consulting fees for three months, and $90,000 per month thereafter on a month-to-month basis. This was an incredible amount of money just to pick our brain and kick the tires. We were ecstatic!

A month later, my dad died of a massive heart attack at the age of 66. This was a tremendous blow to our company and to me. Western Union had scheduled several people to visit us the day after Dad died, and they called to see if I would like to reschedule the meeting. I said "Absolutely not!" I didn't want to show any weakness, so we had the meeting as planned. Dad would've been proud of me, and news of my stiff upper lip traveled quickly through Western Union's top and middle management.

I put on a good front, but I was crushed. I had a special relationship with Dad, and would miss him. We had worked together for twenty-four years, and regularly used each other as a sounding board. We could talk frankly about anything, and had lunch together almost every day. We used to argue a lot, each of us intensely trying to make our point, but it was healthy most of the time. Our employees adored Dad and were sad to see him go.

Dad had a history of heart trouble but was a tough old boot and seemed invincible. But I should've seen it coming. The day before he died, he told me not to make reservations for him for the upcoming National Check Cashers Association convention in October. I was shocked. Dad always went to the convention. We made a fun trip out of it by taking our wives. I insisted Dad go to the convention. He said, "Goddamn, son. Can't you just do what I say for once, without arguing?" I was baffled: that kind of response was not like him. Dad was always up for a good argument.

The next day, he had a long talk with me about running the business. He gave me his insights on the different strengths and weaknesses of our key people, and shared his views on many things. It seemed to be a strange conversation, but I enjoyed it.

I learned later he had spent the entire day shaking hands and thanking our people for the good job they had done over the years. He went to visit Jim Paul, our outside construction contractor, who was working on one of the locations. Jim grew up in San Pedro and was a good friend of our family and mine. He built or remodeled every Nix location and would later come to work with us full time to be our project manager and supervise our warehouse, facilities, and maintenance. Jim worked with us for almost thirty years. Dad thanked him for everything he had done to support our company's success, and for being a person we could count on no matter what.

Dad then met with Darline at the main office for about two hours. They talked about many things and reminisced about old times. He told Darline, who was a district manager at the time, that it was time for her to take on more responsibility, and to team up with me in a better way. He asked her to stop doing her passive resistant thing with me and instead to stand her ground when she didn't agree with something I was doing. She promised she would. He thanked her for being a special part of the team and our family for the past twenty-two years.

That night, Dad told Mom what a great wife she was, and that she meant everything to him. Then, they went out to dinner with Pam's parents, Cliff and Margaret Harvey, to celebrated Dad's sixty-sixth birthday, which was that day. Dad and my father-in-law Cliff had become best friends ever since Pam and I got married in 1970. Dad thanked him for his friendship and the trust he placed in us by loaning us a large sum of money years earlier on a handshake. They had a nice evening together.

About an hour after returning home that night, my mom heard a loud crashing noise coming from the bathroom. Dad was lying dead on the floor, bleeding from the fall he had taken. He had a major coronary heart attack that killed him instantly.

It was a difficult time, as it always is when a loved one passes away. It was especially difficult for me because he was also my business partner and mentor. The circumstances of his death amaze me to this day. How many of us get to bid farewell to the people we love and care about, then make the transition without a long debilitating illness? It is the way I'd like to go when it is my time (hopefully when I am very old).

Western Union continued to use our consulting services

on a month-to-month basis until May of 1991. I was thrilled to be making $90,000 per month, but was anxious to strike a deal that would allow us to grow the business. We had managed to open three more branches while we were searching for capital, but it was just too slow.

In October or November of 1990, the president of American Express Money Order Division, Charlie Fote, invited me to see the Los Angeles Raiders play the Denver Broncos in their private spectator box at Mile High Stadium. Charlie planned to give me the details of their offer to invest $10 million in our company.

I told Western Union I was going to the game, so if they planned on making an offer, they needed to do it quickly. They said they wanted to team up with us, and felt it would happen soon, but they were not ready to make an offer.

To my surprise, they offered us a $1 million "break-off fee" to not do the deal with American Express, and give them an exclusive right to negotiate. They said the break-off fee meant that if we failed to come to an agreement that was satisfactory to both parties, Western Union would pay us $1 million. I thought, "Wow, what an endorsement." I signed the document before going to the game. There, I told Charlie I'd signed an exclusive right to negotiate with Western Union, but hoped we could revisit his idea if things didn't pan out. He was not happy.

CHAPTER 6

WUNIX

In June of 1991, Western Union and Nix Check Cashing created a joint venture company called Wunix, Inc. It was a very exciting time! We now had the vehicle to build the first nationwide check-cashing company. Customers would be able to use their check-cashing card coast-to-coast to get fast, friendly, courteous service at a fair and reasonable price, from locations that were clean, well-maintained, and professionally staffed with people who lived right in their own community. The Nix business model would become the industry standard across the country.

We also planned to add banking services, to give consumers the freedom to choose the services that best fit their needs. Traditional banking services would be conveniently offered in low- to moderate-income communities, allowing us to compete for the consumers who were using banks to conduct their financial affairs.

We planned to create an attractive franchise program for the thousands of check cashers that were already Western Union money transfer agents. All of us would benefit from the $30 million per year advertising program that was in place at Western Union at the time. It was a fabulous strategy.

We planned to open ten stores in Northern California as our Phase One, with a planned national rollout of at least five hundred company stores and hundreds of franchising stores for our Phase Two. Nix Check Cashing had an exclusive five-county territory in Los Angeles, Orange County, Riverside, San Bernardino, and Ventura, and would sell to Western Union during Phase Two.

We decided to name the stores "Gold Star Check-Cashing," and created a beautiful logo and signage. Nix Check Cashing was in charge of running Wunix/Gold Star Check-Cashing, and Western Union contributed the capital. We had a five-person board: Jim Calvano, CEO of Western Union; Ed Furhman, President of Western Union; Mark Perlberg, Senior VP of Western Union; Ray Parry, Vice President of Nix Check Cashing and Wunix; and myself, President of Nix Check Cashing and Wunix.

I proudly announced our plans to the check cashers who attended the California Check Cashers Association meeting in Northern California. A few days later, I received a call from Dave Robinson, the owner of two stores in the Bay Area, who was very excited about our program. He was interested in becoming a franchisee of Wunix, but the program wasn't ready yet, and we decided to meet and discuss the possibility of purchasing his two stores, with Dave coming aboard as our site locator and construction manager.

I flew to Oakland and toured his two stores. They were perfect! Both of them were stand-alone locations that used to be fast food restaurants, and they looked just like a Nix Check Cashing location. Dave was a professional business-man, and we hit it off really well, too. This was a fabulous opportunity for both of us. We agreed on a fair price for his two stores, subject to the approval of Western Union.

The Wunix business plan anticipated opening new stores rather than acquiring existing stores, but this was too good to pass up. It was a perfect fit. I called Western Union and excitedly told them about this great opportu-nity to kick-start Phase One of our business. They thought it was a good price compared to a *de novo* startup, but it wasn't the plan. I agreed it wasn't the plan, but insisted that we take advantage of this unexpected opportunity, and they reluctantly agreed. We purchased both of Dave Robinson's stores, and he came on as our site locator and construction manager.

We had a number of situations arise over the next couple of years where I felt we should shift gears and they didn't, even when they agreed it would probably be a good idea. Jim Calvano explained to me one day that Western Union was a "process-driven management culture," and Nix was an "event-driven management culture." I had never looked at it that way before. I immediately understood why it was sometimes difficult to get on the same page.

I was lucky to be working with terrific people at Western Union. Jim and I had a fabulous relationship, and I thought the world of him. He was an extremely smart, savvy, tough, experienced businessman who grew up in Chicago. Jim was about ten years older than I was, but we had a strong connection. Mark Perlberg was our direct contact, and was also an amazing businessman. He was about ten years younger, but we also connected very well and became good friends. He was an attorney who'd become an entrepreneur at a very young age. He and his partner built a successful bill payment company and sold it to Western Union a couple years prior to our Wunix deal. Customers of the check-cashing industry pay their bills by purchasing money orders and mailing them or by paying cash to a check casher, who would use a bill payment company to electronically pay the bill on behalf of the customer. It was an excellent service, and a natural expansion of the Western Union product offering.

The National Check Cashers Association annual convention was held in San Diego in October of 1991, just four months after we launched Wunix DBA Gold Star Check-Cashing. Western Union was a primary sponsor of the convention each year, and always made a presentation. This year, we would use this opportunity to officially share our exciting strategy with the industry, most of whom were money transfer agents who could benefit from the attractive franchise program we planned to offer. We knew there were grumblings from the industry about Western Union teaming up with Nix Check Cashing in this way, but we were positive that most of the industry would see it in a positive light, once we had an opportunity to share our vision.

I had been approached a month earlier by the chairman of the Board of Directors of the National Check Cashers Association, Ray Mustafa, who asked me to resign my vice president position. I was shocked and offended. I had a good relationship with the board members, was one of the founders of the organization, and together, we had built the association to about two thousand members in only five years. I asked Ray why he wanted me to resign. He said that teaming up with a major industry supplier like Western Union was unacceptable. I told him I had done nothing wrong, and that Wunix was a business opportunity that any of our members would take. On top of that, it would be good for our industry, because it would bring credibility and expand the market for our services. Our members would have a chance to participate as a franchisee and grow their own business within the Gold Star Check Cashing network.

He said, "Everyone is upset with you, and we want you to resign." I indignantly said no. "I'm proud of what I've done," I told him, "and I will run for re-election."

The convention was held in San Diego that year, and there were about a thousand attendees. We began presenting our business strategy to a hostile audience. During the Q-and-A period that followed our presentation, some of the business people were yelling and screaming obscenities at us. We'd been set up. Industry leaders had planted people in the audience to disrupt us. It was a horrible experience for the Western Union executives on the stage and for me.

The next morning was the election, and I lost by a landslide, about fourteen hundred to a hundred forty votes.

I quit the association with a lot of resentment. I felt what they did was not right. But things were about to get much worse. The industry formed a new organization called the National Money Transmitters Association, with the distinct purpose of suing Western Union. They raised a significant amount of money and filed a lawsuit against Western Union for predatory business practices. They claimed Western Union would use their financial statements, which they had for each money transfer agent, to target the good locations to open a Gold Star Check Cashing store. They also threatened Western Union with a boycott, which would have crippled their money transfer network.

In the meantime, Charlie Fote, CEO of American Express Integrated Payment Systems, had started a new money transfer company called MoneyGram, and was flying all over the country to chat up the check-cashing associations. He told them that American Express would never team up with an industry member and create competition like Western Union had done. He encouraged everyone to switch to MoneyGram. This was done while American Express was also funding the growth of another check-cashing company, America's Cash Express, known as "ACE." They were ruthlessly trying to capitalize on the discontent within the industry.

About a year later, Dave Robinson was putting the finishing touches on our new Gold Star Check Cashing location in Richmond, California. A very large white man who didn't seem like he was from the neighborhood approached Dave in the parking lot. He told Dave not to open the store for business, and said if he did, he would pay the ultimate price. Dave asked, "What do you mean?" and the guy said, "You know what I mean. If you open this store, we'll deal with you Chicago style."

Dave called me in a panic, and I told him to call

Richmond Police Department to make a police report. We opened the store for business a couple of days later. Over the following several days, the thug from Chicago went to each of our stores and intimidated our employees. Our employees had eggs thrown at them when they left work. Then two of our locations had a pipe thrown through the plate glass window while they were open for business and had customers in the lobby. We made a police report of all of the incidents as they occurred, but we needed a better way to protect our people.

I met with Mark Virgo, owner of the contract security company used by Nix Check Cashing, and explained the situation at Gold Star Check Cashing. I asked him if he would go to Northern California to protect our people, and he said of course. Mark was a big, tough black man who grew up in South Central Los Angeles. Nothing scared him. I told him I didn't want him to break any laws, but I wanted the Chicago thugs to know we were not afraid of them. Their intimidation tactics were not going to work with us. He agreed and drove to Northern California with one of his biggest and toughest employees, Mark Henry.

A few days later, Dave and I attended the California Check Cashers Association meeting at the Holiday Inn in Oakland, California. Dave and I were dressed in suits and ties, and many of the hundred or so participants were wearing sport coats. The Chicago thug arrived wearing a sweat suit, and immediately walked up to Dave and punched him in the face with his fist. Dave is a physically small man, and no match for this giant thug, but I was. I quickly went to Dave's rescue and traded a few punches, until a number of the check cashers in the room pulled us apart.

Oakland Police Department arrived, and took both of our statements. I told the officers what was going on, and flashed my sheriff's badge, which was clearly marked Lieutenant. The retired part was not as noticeable. The officers quickly called their watch commander, who came to the scene with several other patrol cars. I told him I wanted the asshole arrested. He agreed, but said they had to interview the other witnesses.

They interviewed most of the hundred check-cashing store owners while I waited outside at the patrol car. Finally, the watch commander came out and said, "Tom, we have a problem. Half of the witnesses say you started the fight, so if we arrest him, we are going to have to arrest you." I said, "Okay, then. Arrest us both."

We were both cited for assault and battery, and released at the scene. They made the thug leave the premises, and I was allowed to go back and attend the meeting. I was amazed that half of the room felt so threatened by Gold Star Check Cashing that they would lie about what had happened.

Early the next morning, I called Jim Calvano. Jim made it very clear early on that he did not want any surprises or to be caught flat-footed. I told Jim the story, and he said, "You did the right thing, Tom. If we're in for a penny, we're in for a pound." I was so glad to be working with a guy who knew there was no turning the cheek to a school-yard bully.

A few days later, I got a call from Mark Virgo, who related the following story. He'd gotten a call from the Gold Star Check Cashing branch in Richmond, telling him that the thug was back in their lobby, making threats. Mark and his partner drove to the location and confronted the thug. They placed him in handcuffs and called the Richmond Police Department. Two officers arrived, and Mark presented them with a detailed incident report of all of the situations that had occurred.

The officers then asked the thug for his side of the story. He said he was driving down the nearby freeway when he started getting a flat tire, so pulled off the freeway and into our parking lot to change his tire. He showed the officers a flat tire on one of his rear wheels. He said he noticed that he had stopped in the parking lot of a check-cashing store so decided to go in and buy a $5 money order before changing his tire. He showed the officers a $5 money order from Gold Star Check Cashing. He said these two security officers from Gold Star Check Cashing falsely arrested him and he wanted to file charges against them.

The two police officers looked at Mark, and, in a knowing way, said, "We have another call, but we will be back to resolve this problem. We suggest you take this man inside and have a talk with him before we get back."

Mark brought the man into the Gold Star Check Cashing location. All of our locations had a double-door entry system, which resembled a hallway with a door on each end. Branch personnel would buzz the outside door to let a person who was authorized to enter the store into the hallway. The inner door was a bulletproof security door with a small bulletproof window that was used to make sure no unauthorized persons came in the mantrap. Once the outer door was closed and locked, the inner door would be opened to allow entry to the teller area of the location. It was a perfect place to have a private conversation.

Richmond Police Department returned and the thug begged them to arrest him. He said he was sent out here from Chicago to intimidate Gold Star Check Cashing employees and admitted to all of the recent incidents. He said he punched a hole in his tire with a screwdriver from his trunk and showed it to the officers. He said he did that to give him the excuse to hang around our location for a while and the $5 money order was another part of his excuse. The officers gladly took him to jail.

The National Check Cashers Association annual

meeting was scheduled for a couple of weeks later in New Orleans. I had planned on taking Ray Parry, Darline Gavin, Dave Robinson, and our regional manager for Northern California, Bob Vizcarra, along with our spouses. Then, I got word that I was to be assassinated at the convention. Someone had put a hit on me.

I decided that Dave Robinson, Bob Vizcarra, and I would go without our spouses and would each have a bodyguard. Ray pleaded with me not to go. He said our business plans were not worth dying for. I said, "I have to go, because once we start running, we'll never be able to stop." Darline, on the other hand, begged me to let her go with me. I said, "Absolutely not. Ray will need you to help him run the business if I am killed. The business needs you, and I cannot risk getting you hurt."

I happened to be meeting with Jerrold Smith, our marketing consultant, a few days later, and told him the situation. We'd become good friends since we began working together in the mid-'80s. He asked me if he could go to the convention with us. He said it would be good to learn more about the industry, and anyway, he "didn't want to miss a good shootout." Jerrold grew up in a rough part of Los Angeles and knew how to handle himself, and the notion that white boys from Chicago would come to town to push us around was repulsive to him.

At Nix, over 90 percent of our management and staff

were African American or Hispanic. This was a result of my commitment to hire people from the communities we served. It was the right thing to do. We had tremendous support from our customer base, which numbered in the hundreds of thousands. Plus, most minority people who lived in Greater Los Angeles and listened to urban or Hispanic radio stations had heard our advertisements for years. They knew we hired from the community, supported worthwhile community causes, had our own scholarship program, a monumental annual food drive, and treated people fairly. It was a common myth that the owner of Nix Check Cashing was a black man, and many people, including Jerrold, were shocked to discover I was white, when they met me for the first time. Our employees had a strong sense of ownership. We were a fabulous team of people.

I was extremely complimented by, and grateful for, Jerrold's offer, and gave him a hug and told him so.

So, eight of us would go to the convention: Dave Robinson, Bob Vizcarra, Jerrold, and me, and a bodyguard for each of us. My brother Jim drove up to be my bodyguard. I was in good hands with Jim. He was a big guy who, like me, grew up fighting in San Pedro, and he brought an arsenal of weapons with him from his home in Parker, Arizona. Pete Currenti, our director of security, Mark Virgo, and Mark Henry would be the other bodyguards.

We would all be armed, except Dave and Bob, and everyone would wear bulletproof vests under our business suits,
except Jerrold and me. I was not about to show any fear or
weakness, and Jerrold was just hardheaded and refused to
wear one.

Mark Virgo had about thirty security guards who
worked for him and protected Nix Check Cashing. These
were rough-and-tumble guys, not the normal, feeble,
private guards that you might find at a grocery store or
bank in a middle-class neighborhood. These folks knew
hundreds of guys from the neighborhood who would step
up, if necessary, to fight the Chicago mob. We could put
together an army. I hoped it wouldn't be necessary, but if
they wanted to play hardball with us, it would be game on!

Pete Currenti was director of security for Nix Check
Cashing. He was also a reserve police officer for the Culver
City Police Department, and an extremely good cop. He
contacted New Orleans Police Department and laid out
the situation. The fact that I was a retired cop didn't hurt
matters. They appreciated the heads-up and gave us their
unofficial blessings.

We arrived at Los Angeles International Airport with
our guns in our luggage and flew to New Orleans. We
picked up our luggage and rental cars, and then stopped
at a different hotel than where the convention was being
held, and ate a late lunch. We talked things over, and then,

separately, we each went to the lobby restroom with our luggage and retrieved our gun, holster, vest, and ammo. One by one they came out of the bathroom looking awesome! I thought to myself, "The Chicago guys are fucking with the wrong people."

We drove to the convention hotel and the eight of us walked into the registration area. I had my big salesman, super-friendly smile, as if nothing was wrong. One of the kingpins of the Chicago check-cashing industry immediately walked up to me and poked me in the chest with his finger three times saying, "Wow! I am surprised you're not wearing a bulletproof vest." This is a common way to finger the target of a hit, although I am not sure that was what he was doing. He may have done it to scare me. I gave him a big smile and said, "I don't need one." Then we marched into the exhibit hall.

We spent that evening and the next day attending all of the meetings and events. I was warm and friendly with everyone, as I normally am at these kinds of events, but we stayed together as a group. Our posse was quite a sight and got attention from everyone at the convention, including Western Union. I can only imagine what they were thinking.

The second night, there was a scheduled cruise on the Mississippi River. A couple of my guys suggested that we skip this event, but that was out of the question. We were not going to show any weakness or fear, and in reality, I had none. It was an exhilarating experience for me and I was having fun. My days as a sheriff, working in the Firestone Park and Watts area of Los Angeles, had prepared me very well for this type of thing. I was ready and able to deal with whatever happened.

I was sitting outside of the riverboat in the warm night air talking with Jerrold, with the rest of my guys a safe distance away. A man walked up to me and nervously asked if I would be willing to come inside and talk to one of the Chicago guys. "I mean, without your muscle," he said. My guys objected, but I said, "Okay, I'll be right in."

Inside, I said hello to the man who had asked to see me. He said, "Tom, you have made your point, and we've decided we don't want to go any further down this road. We've all talked, and we don't want to go back to the old days. Let's just get back to competing in the marketplace." I said, "That is what I prefer, but I will play this game however you want to play it. I will have hundreds of guys from Compton and Los Angeles breathing down your throat, if that's what you want." He said, "We understand that, Tom, and we don't want to go there. You have my word that you will have no more problems. Your guys can put away their guns and take off their bulletproof vests and enjoy the rest of the convention." We shook on it.

I was ecstatic! I was glad they didn't want gangland

warfare, and I felt I could trust his word and handshake. That night, I met with my team at the hotel and told them the story. They were not convinced, and weren't keen on taking off their guns and bulletproof vests. I was pretty sure everything would be okay. I had a reputation for saying what I mean and doing what I say, and the Chicago guys knew they would definitely have a battle on their hands if they didn't live up to their promise. I decided that everyone would take off their vests, and only Pete and I would carry concealed weapons. I carried my OMC 380 backup, which was in a wallet holster and completely undetectable. Pete had a snub-nose .38 in a shoulder holster under his sport coat, which was also difficult to see. It was important for the Chicago boys to see that we took them at their word, and intended to live up to our end of the bargain.

We enjoyed the next day at the convention, although some of the guys were nervous. That night, we all went out to a nice restaurant in the French Quarter to celebrate. We finished off the evening by hitting every single strip bar on Bourbon Street. We walked home together around 3 a.m., laughing and joking and bonding. I've always felt a special sense of gratitude for those guys who stood by my side during those stressful, dangerous times.

Dave Robinson finished opening all of the Gold Star Check Cashing stores a short time later, without incident. We never ever experienced a single threat from the

Chicago types or anyone else. They kept their word.

Dave agreed to come on as our VP of Franchising, and moved to Southern California. He also took over management of TND Security Products division. We were both extremely excited to be teaming up in a stronger way. Dave proved to be a fabulous addition to our team and made a significant contribution to the success of our company. We also became very close friends.

Gold Star Check Cashing's volume grew slower than we expected. We modeled our growth based on the experience we had opening a Nix Check Cashing location, but shaved off a little, since outside of Southern California, we didn't have a well-known brand name or existing pool of card-carrying customers. We also discovered the demographics were not as strong for check-cashing customers in the Bay Area. Everyone was disappointed.

I had argued early on not to create a forecast and budget for the pilot stores. I felt we should do our best, and evaluate the results. If they were satisfactory, we could do more stores. If they weren't, we could make changes to the model, in pricing and marketing and a host of other things, to see if we could obtain acceptable performance. I did not want us to be saddled with a budget that might cloud the issues or hamper our flexibility to make changes.

But big companies live and die by their budgets, and it was unthinkable to Western Union for us to do business without one. They said, "How will we know if we're doing well or not without a budget?" I said, "We have a new name and a new territory with different dynamics. Let's just evaluate the results, then decide next steps." I could not convince them.

As I feared, scads of people at Western Union scrutinized every line item in the budget for each branch. We were pressured to make budget, instead of doing what we thought would be best for the pilot. I wholeheartedly support the budget process for ongoing business, and we had an excellent budgeting system at Nix Check Cashing. But, when Nix created a pilot to launch a new product, or changed hours or pricing, we did it without a budget. We would select five branches to test our new approach, and let them run with the ball. Their objective was to figure out how to make it work, or find out that it didn't. We wanted them to keep their eye on the goal, without worrying too much about a nitpicking accountant waving a flag at their every decision.

In spite of the frustration and disappointment, Gold Star Check Cashing became moderately successful, though it was pretty clear that a Phase Two national rollout was unlikely.

To make matters worse, Jim Calvano was suddenly terminated. It was a blow to him and me, and I believe it was a horrible mistake for Western Union.

Not long after that, Western Union wound up in bankruptcy court. Charlie Fote, from American Express, was running a spinoff company called First Data, and he wanted to buy Western Union in the worst way. But it temporarily got away from him. A company called First Financial, headquartered in Atlanta, Georgia, beat him out. First Data later purchased First Financial, and Fote finally had his hands on Western Union.

This string of events put us in a position to purchase Western Union's interest in Gold Star Check Cashing. We were excited to be running our own company again.

CHAPTER 7

1992 Riots

On Wednesday, April 29, 1992, I returned to my room at the Holiday Inn in Oakland, California about 10:30 p.m. I'd just come from a California Check Cashers Association meeting. I called home to say good night to Pam and she was in tears.

The Los Angeles riot had started a few hours earlier, after a jury acquitted the four police officers accused in the beating of Rodney King. The city was lit up with looting, arson, theft, and violence, and the worst of it all was right in the heart of Nixland.

The next morning, I flew to Los Angeles and was horrified to see fires spread all over South Central as we made our approach to LAX. It was a lot worse than I'd imagined. I had arranged to meet with my leadership team when I returned, and they were all waiting for me in our upstairs conference room: Ray Parry, vice president;

Darline Gavin, who was regional manager at the time; Pete Currenti, security director; Ricky Floyd, district manager; and Dwight Cervantes, district manager. The problem was we had people, and a lot of cash, spread out at all of our branches throughout the regions of the riots.

We watched television news reporting and reviewed the information we'd received from our branches. It was clear the riot was picking up steam, and it would not be safe for our people to remain in the locations. We decided to close all of the stores. We had been a seven-day-a-week business since we started the company in 1966. Closing the stores was uncomfortable, but it was the right thing to do.

We knew our locations would be left unprotected at a time when the Los Angeles Police Department was powerless to stop people from burning and looting. We also had an unusually large amount of cash at the branches, because it was the day before May 1. Since welfare recipients used to receive their checks in the mail on the first and fifteenth of each month, we always had a lot of cash on hand on those days. So the riots hit at a particularly unlucky time for us.

Each of our locations had two safes. The first was a floor safe, cemented into the concrete floor and almost impossible to break into or remove. We stored all the large bills in this safe. The other safe was an upright safe, bolted to the floor. It was strong, but not as secure as the floor safe.

We used the upright safe to store rolled coins, smaller bills, and other assets like bus passes.

Unfortunately, the floor safe was not large enough to hold all of the large bills we kept on the first and the fifteenth of the month, so we had to rely on the upright safe to store the overflow. This left us way too vulnerable to the rioters. (After the riots, we installed huge floor safes at each location that could hold all of the valuables and were impossible to break into.)

We had to pick up the cash! We decided to put four armed security guards in each of our armored trucks, with Ricky in one truck and Dwight in the other. We also had a chase car with two more security agents following each armored truck. They would provide extra protection in case the trucks came under attack. The objective was to pick up the cash, the money orders, and the shotguns.

Each of our locations was equipped with a double-barrel shotgun with a short barrel. Our branch management had regular training on how to use them, just in case a car rammed into the side of the building or someone with a sledgehammer began breaking their way through the bulletproof glass that separated the teller area from the customer lobby area. It was also part of our new employee orientation. We wanted our people to feel safe at work, and we also wanted to get the word out to the criminal community that they would be ill-advised to try something at a Nix Check Cashing location.

We also wanted criminals to know about the time-delay system on our safes. The safe would not open until thirty minutes after the combination had been performed. This procedure was designed to keep our assets and our people safe, because criminals weren't very likely to rob a location where they had to sit and wait for thirty minutes to get their loot.

But during the riots, the thirty-minute time delay was a big problem for our security teams. It meant that, during a time of complete lawlessness, the team had to wait for thirty minutes at each branch while surrounding businesses were being looted and burned. It gave the serious criminals time to get guns and attack when our guys carried the money through the "kill zone," the distance between the branch and the armored car.

We planned for each armored truck to pick up cash from three or four branches, then drive back to our main office in Carson to unload. We didn't want to take the risk of having one of our trucks robbed while carrying too much cash.

I had four guys to protect the main office, in addition to Pete and myself. Two guys from our IT department were willing to stay, Brett Wilson and Steve Corbin, and one of our branch managers, Johnny Williams. We also had Joe McIntire, the husband of Lily McIntire in our accounting department, volunteer to help. Darline and Lilia Clark were downstairs, counting the money as it came in and preparing it to be deposited into the bank. The cash for each store had to be kept separate, because each branch was owned by different limited partnerships.

Normally we kept no money at the main office, and there was no mention of Nix Check Cashing on the sign. We didn't want the Nix Check Cashing logo ever to give someone the idea that we kept cash on hand in the office. Now we were using it to store all of our cash.

The office was only vulnerable from the front and back, unless someone burrowed through the side walls or tried to come through the roof. We had wrought iron protecting the front windows and entry door. My office was upstairs, with windows that gave a clear view of the parking lot. I had an AR-15 assault rifle, our only rifle. There were plenty of handguns and double-barreled shotguns, but they were only effective at a close range. The back of the building had no windows, just a large garage door that opened to allow our armored trucks to drive into the loading bay, and a four-foot solid door people used to enter the back of our building.

We parked our armored van across the rear parking lot, positioned so Joe, sitting lookout in the van, could see the back doors and alert us if we came under attack from the back.

Early in the afternoon, a reporter spotted our armored truck and crew at our location at Martin Luther King and

Vermont, and this led the news station to speculate, on air, about the reasons behind the rampant looting of the mini-malls. "It just occurred to us," the news anchor said, "a lot of these mini-malls have check-cashing locations in them." The station went on to describe how each location was loaded with cash and other valuable commodities, such as food stamps, money orders, lottery tickets, and bus passes. I know they meant no harm, but it felt to us like they were pointing rioters in our direction.

Things got hectic. I received reports from the field that some of our upright safes were missing. I later found out that a tow truck had been seen dragging a safe out of a location with a chain. It used its hydraulic lift to hoist the safe onto the back of the truck, and drove off. All in all, we lost seven upright safes, containing about $300,000 in uninsured cash.

When our security team arrived at our location on Washington Boulevard and Maple Street, it was burning. We had them go back later that night to retrieve the cash. They found the store had been burned out on the inside, and then drenched from the fire department, putting out the blaze. The safe was full of water, with the bundles of money soaking inside. Each bill had to be pulled from each bundle and dried with a hair dryer.

When our team arrived at our branch on Vernon and Main, they discovered two men jack-hammering the floor safe out of the concrete floor. We found the same thing happening at our location in Compton. We couldn't get the cash out of these damaged safes, so I stationed some men to stand guard over those locations.

About 10 p.m. Thursday night, I received a call from the security guards I had posted at the Compton branch, because someone was shooting automatic weapon fire at the building. I called the Police Department and explained the situation. They told me there was no one available to respond, so we were on our own. I sent one of the armored trucks to go and rescue those men. The truck pulled up next to the building and swung the door open. All three guards jumped safely inside, and the truck drove away.

About half an hour later, I got a call from the guards at Vernon and Main. Snipers had positioned themselves on the rooftops of nearby buildings and were shooting. This time, neither of our armored trucks were available to rescue those guys. I decided to send Joe and Johnny in our armored van. Unfortunately, Joe had been listening to the radio as he sat in the armored van guarding the rear of the building, and the van's battery was dead. Our guys were at risk in the field, and we had to delay to jump-start the van. Fortunately, we rescued our guys a short time later. The rioters were never able to get the floor safe out of the cement, but the building was set on fire and completely gutted.

It was an extremely stressful and dreadful night. We heard on the news that the riot was spreading closer to our main office in Carson, where we were holed up with our cash. The Alpha Beta Supermarket on Avalon Boulevard was burning, just a couple miles from us. Several times, we saw cars full of men drive through our parking lot very slowly, looking for easy pickings.

Then, a car stopped right in front of our main office, and four armed men got out. I was perched upstairs, peering down through the window with my rifle in the ready position. I took a moment to call Pete on the intercom, and told him it looked like we had trouble. Pete and one of the other guys came up and positioned themselves at the other windows, so we covered the entire wall facing the parking lot. The men outside talked and pointed at our building. They were obviously considering the option of breaking in. I don't think they saw us, but they evidently decided not to do it, and got in their car and drove away.

My sons Tom and Bill, who were teenagers at the time, called and asked if they could come down and help protect the family business. I told them I wanted them to stay at our home in Fountain Valley, to protect their mom and my mom, who had come to stay with us for safety reasons. I told them to get the guns I kept at home, just in case. I didn't know how far the riot might reach, and I was also worried about someone targeting my family for kidnap and ransom.

I called my brother, Jim, who lived in Parker, Arizona and asked him to come help me. We needed more ammo and rifles to adequately protect ourselves. We also needed food, and I wanted Jim to ride with me in the armored truck in the morning, when we made the run to deposit all of the cash we'd picked up from the branches.

We would definitely be out of business if the armored truck were robbed on the way to the bank, because we didn't have anywhere near enough insurance to cover the amount of money in the truck. I worried about an inside job. One of the contract security guards or someone they knew could plan an ambush to rob the truck. I wanted to deliver the cash to the bank myself, because I was the captain and was willing to go down with the ship if necessary. Bobby Williams, a longtime trusted employee, would drive the armored truck. Jim and I would be in the back compartment with all the money, heavily armed.

It took Jim four hours to drive to Carson, so I had to wait. About 3 a.m. Friday morning, we finished picking up all the cash from the branches, and it was ready to be deposited. All of my men were safely out of the field. The rest of my employees were home and not scheduled to come back to work until Monday. There was nothing more to do except get the cash back to the bank.

Everyone at the main office was exhausted. I arranged to have two contract security guards come in, so I could let the rest of the team go home. But only one guard showed up, and I had never seen him before. Here I was with a truckload of money and just one single armed man I'd never met. I got the creepy feeling that this was a really bad circumstance.

I called Jim and asked him to be careful when he got to the main office. Then, I grabbed three cushions off the upstairs couch and settled into the armored car to wait for Jim. The guard was instructed to get me whenever Jim arrived.

I was completely exhausted and completely stressed out. I placed the cushions between the piles of plastic garbage bags, stuffed with money, and lay down to take a nap. It was at least a hundred degrees in that truck. I stripped down to my boxers, but I was still sweating. My body ached and my head was throbbing. I couldn't sleep, even though I'd been up for forty-five hours.

I finally drifted into a deep sleep, only to be woken a short time later by the guard, banging on the steel truck door. He told me there was someone at the door to the office. I could not see clearly but finally made out that it was the second guard, the one who hadn't shown up earlier. I prayed that this was not a setup, and bent over to unlock the door.

The second guard apologized for being late, and I shook his hand and thanked him for coming. I was relieved.

These two guards had had a chance to try something, and they didn't take it. I was now confident that my security team had no malicious intentions. I got back into the armored sauna bath, and lay back down on the cushions. I still couldn't sleep, but I could rest a little easier.

Jim arrived about 5 a.m. I called our driver, Bobby Williams, and asked him to come down and drive the armored truck. It was time.

We were prepared for trouble, but we had no incidents on the way to the bank. We deposited the money safely, which was a huge relief. Things had gone so smoothly, I asked Bobby and Jim if they were willing to take a tour of our branches, and they both agreed.

When we arrived at each branch, Jim and I would jump out of the truck, me with my semi-automatic AR-15, similar to the weapons used by the military in Vietnam, and Jim with his modified M1 automatic. Bobby stayed in the cab of the truck, prepared to defend us through its gun ports if necessary. It felt good to have him watching our back.

Branch after branch was in shambles. Windows and computer terminals smashed, some of the equipment and office furniture stolen, papers strewn everywhere. Some of the bullet-resistant glass was damaged, and entry doors were knocked off their hinges. It was an incredibly disheartening sight. We passed block after block of retail buildings burnt to the ground, many still smoldering. We saw burned-out cars in the middle of the street, and heard occasional gunshots in the distance. It was a war zone. Nixland was in ruins.

However, I was amazed to see a number of our branches were not set on fire, even though they were located in shopping centers that were burned to the ground. I found out later that many of our loyal customers had come to our defense during the riot because they didn't want "their" check-cashing store destroyed. They could not stop the looting, but they stopped the burning. We even had a gang member call us shortly after the riot. He said he had always been treated with respect at Nix, and his gang decided not to burn Nix because we were part of the community. This was a highly unusual endorsement, but it was heartfelt and I took it that way. I was grateful that our good reputation and relationship with the community had saved our business. Doing things right, treating people fairly, and supporting worthwhile community programs for decades had paid off in a way we'd never expected.

By about 10:30 Friday morning, I was in my car, on the way home. I was numb and completely exhausted, but not sleepy. I wondered if our business would be able to survive this blow. I wondered how long it would take for the riot to end. I was thankful that none of our people were injured or killed, and that my family was safe. I knew life was a great adventure, but I wished this were part of the adventure that I could have missed.

I gave Pam a big hug and kiss when I got home. She

asked me, "What's going to happen?" I said, "I don't know, but we'll figure it out." Then I went to bed.

About two hours later, Pam woke me and said Los Angeles City Councilman Mark Ridley Thomas was trying to reach me. The city wanted us to reopen our chain immediately.

I told them it was out of the question. We couldn't open our stores during a riot. Ridley's deputy explained that the city needed Nix Check Cashing to open up because people had nowhere to cash their checks. Many of the liquor stores, markets, check cashers, and banks had been burned down, and the ones that hadn't were closed. "We need people to get access to cash, so we can start to calm things down. We need you to open up, as a friend of the city."

I said, "I understand that, but I cannot and will not put my people's safety in jeopardy."

The deputy asked what it would take to get us to reopen. My main concern was safety. I said I could have all of my employees report to our main office in Carson, if the city could provide a police escort for them to safely enter each branch, and then escort them out of the branch again at night.

I also needed a way to keep my people safe once they were in the branch. I said I'd require two police units to escort each armored truck, so they can safely deliver the money we'd need.

Finally, I told him I'd need a lot more cash than we usually keep on hand, if we were going to cash checks for the entire city.

He said okay. "We will provide you with the police escorts you asked for, and we'll station the National Guard at each branch, to keep your people safe. We'll give you a letter of credit from the city, or provide you with funds directly, to make sure you don't run out of cash." I asked if he could guarantee all of this, and he said yes.

Darline and I coordinated with our district mangers and branch managers, to see if we could get enough employees to return to work on such short notice. In less than an hour, I called Ridley's deputy to tell him it was a go.

My wife Pam was beside herself. She told me I was crazy. She said, "You can't trust the city, and you know it." She begged me not to do it, but I knew under the circumstances, I had no other choice. Every challenge or adversity comes with a silver lining, and I was convinced this was it for the riot. It was simply an awesome opportunity. We would come to the aid of the city. We'd gain political credibility, huge marketing exposure, and excellent customer goodwill. New customers would visit Nix Check Cashing, and they'd return to us again and again even after the riot was over. This would be exactly the benefit we'd need to help us come back from the devastation. We had been chosen to rise up out of the ashes.

The deputy was ecstatic. He told me Mark Ridley Thomas was grateful to have us step up in the city's time of need. They immediately put out a news release, announcing Nix Check Cashing would be open 8 a.m. to 5 p.m. Saturday and Sunday. They listed the branches that would be open, and gave our office number to call if people needed more information. Every TV station and urban and Hispanic radio station in Los Angeles started broadcasting this news. The telephone company got a list of the locations that would be open, so their operators could direct people to the appropriate branch without having them call us. The churches in the area announced it to their congregations and the Red Cross agreed to bus people to our locations on Saturday and Sunday. It was a huge deal.

I was energized, but not for long. About 5 p.m., I received a call from Ridley's deputy, telling me that the National Guard could not be arranged. The city could not provide any security for our people once they were in the branches.

I was furious! I told him we had no choice but to open, now that the news media were directing people to our branches. We decided to put a security guard with a shotgun inside of each location, to help protect our people. We needed four security men for each armored truck, and many of Virgo's men were spent after two days protecting our company. We needed more help. Lily's husband Joe, Lilia Clark's husband James, Darline's husband Mitchell, and my cousin Gary Whiting all volunteered to protect the branch personnel. My brother Jim volunteered to work on one of the armored trucks.

About 10 p.m., I received another call from Ridley's deputy. He said the police department was not going to be able to escort our people into the branches. He said the city felt it was more important to have the police guard the workers at the Department of Water and Power, and there was just not enough manpower to go around. I was livid, and reminded him that we were doing the city a favor. The only reason we had decided to reopen our business was because they promised to keep our people safe. He apologized, and said they had done everything possible to try and make it happen.

I told him I could not do it without a police escort of our armored trucks. Our men are relatively safe inside the truck, but the hundred-foot walk from the truck to the mantrap door was a "kill zone," and I was positive that some of our men would be injured, or worse, without police protection. He reassured me that we would have a police escort of our armored trucks.

At 4 a.m., the police showed up to our Carson office, as promised. But about an hour later, I got a call from one of our security men on the truck. He said the police were refusing to follow them to the branches, because it crossed city boundaries.

The captain at the LAPD command post confirmed the order. He said it wasn't his decision. It had come from farther up the chain of command. "It's out of my hands, Tom. There's nothing I can do."

The city had asked us to open in their time of need. This was not a greedy check-cashing company trying to make hay. I believed that this decision would result in the death of innocent people, and I knew the police escort would be a show of force that would keep everyone safe.

I told him of my experience as a deputy sheriff at Firestone Station, and that "clusterfucks" happen all of the time. (When I was in the department, that was how we referred to situations that were mismanaged due to great confusion.) I went on to say, "I know that no one wants to be responsible for giving an order that could have catastrophic consequences for LAPD. But I also know that communication mistakes happen all of the time, and I could really use a communication 'mistake' right now that would give those officers the authority to escort us in."

He said, "Let me see what I can do." About fifteen minutes later, my security man called me from the truck. The police had agreed to escort the truck to each the branches. They were on their way.

Our security teams that day had very different protocols

from usual. We needed to escort our tellers from our main office to each of our locations. We were going to send them out two cars at a time, riding in tandem to the branch, and the security team was to ride shotgun and protect them if necessary. Once in the branch, they were to walk back and forth in the teller area with their shotguns in plain view. I wanted people to know we had protection. They were not to go outside under any circumstances. If they came under attack in any way, they were to shoot to kill. It was a desperate time, and we needed to be prepared to take desperate measures. "You have one purpose," I told them, "and that is to protect our people."

I spoke with our tellers, managers, and district managers, who were assembled at the office. I explained the plan, and told them they would be safe. I complimented them on having the willingness and courage to help the city restore calm. I was proud of them. I thanked them for their loyalty and dedication, and I was positive that our company would recover when this was over, because we were sticking together as a team.

Everyone made it safely into their branch. There were hundreds of people lined up at each location, waiting to cash checks. The people were calm and well-behaved. They seemed to understand that our company was taking the extra step for them, and they were grateful.

About 10 a.m. Saturday morning, I got a call from

Ridley's deputy, who told me they were unable to provide a letter of credit or city funds. That was the final straw! I could not believe what they had done to us. Now our people were in the branches, and I could just imagine what would happen when we ran out of money.

I stood up and nearly passed out. The thought that my decision was putting two hundred of my teammates in harm's way was debilitating. I came unglued. I knew I had to remain calm if I was going to figure out a way to resolve this situation. I went to the bathroom and washed my face. I decided to take a short meditation break. I had been practicing transcendental meditation for twenty minutes twice a day since the early 1970s. It is a profoundly powerful tool that results in centering oneself and creating an environment for ideas to flow into your mind. It worked!

I broke out of my panic, and sprang into action. I called Jerrold Smith, our marketing consultant, and asked him to visit each of the radio stations that he knew, so they could ask their listeners on-air to be patient if we ran short on cash. At KJLH, Jerrold ran into the Reverend Jesse Jackson, and told him our story. He offered to help in any way possible.

I had already withdrawn all of our own funds, so I called Jim Calvano, the CEO of Western Union, and explained the situation. He asked if there was anything he could do to help, and I said "Yes! Wire me $5 million."

He said, "I can't do that!" But we were in a life-or-death situation, and if we ran out of cash, there would have been no way to protect my team from the angry rioters. I told Jim I would sign a document giving him ownership of our entire company, everything I owned personally, and my share of ownership in Wunix, if we failed to pay him back.

He said, "If you're willing to do that, I'll send you the money." He didn't have the authority to transfer that much money, but he did it anyway. The Board of Directors would later call him on the carpet for his actions. He told them, "You put me in charge of doing what I think is best for Western Union and our partner Wunix. Under these circumstances, I stand by my decision." I will always be grateful to Jim for standing by my side.

I called Sanwa Bank and told them to expect a $5 million wire, plus we would be depositing millions of dollars in checks Saturday night so we could withdraw more cash on Sunday morning. But the bank told me they were out of currency, and had no way to get any more from the Federal Reserve, because the armored truck companies were closed during the riot.

I could not believe what was happening. There was a new roadblock at every turn. We could send our trucks to pick up the currency directly from the Fed, but it was Federal Reserve policy not to allow access to private firms like ours. I needed someone to give the Federal Reserve permission to let us in.

I was active politically, and decided to call Assemblywoman Marguerite Archie Hudson. We had gotten to know each other and had mutual respect. She put me in touch with Tom Sayles, California's Secretary of Business, Transportation and Housing in the cabinet of Governor Wilson. He couldn't believe the city had hung us out to dry, and told me he'd try to get me some help.

He called me a short while later. He told me he'd spoken with Governor Wilson, who had spoken with President Bush, and that I would be getting a call from Jim Gillerian, the Superintendent of Banking, and from John Gleason, the senior vice president of the Federal Reserve Bank. They told me we were approved to pick up cash at the Fed, and gave me the details.

We cashed checks without incident over the weekend.

The riot was calming down, and the media said it was over and time to rebuild LA. In actuality, the violence continued for several weeks. Our security team was involved in three separate shootouts in the weeks following the official "end" of the riot. None of our people were hurt, but two criminals were shot and killed.

We had several other robbery attempts, including one of José Jimenez, our assistant director of security. José was making a small cash transfer from our branch at Figueroa and Imperial. When he walked out of the mantrap, he noticed two gang member types watching him from a car across the street. José pulled out of the lot and saw the car pull out behind him. When José stopped at a red light, the man in the passenger side of the car jumped out with a gun in his hand and started running towards José. José was watching in the rearview mirror, and punched the accelerator, driving through the intersection. The gang-banger jumped back in the car and chased José onto the freeway at high speed for about ten miles, until José caught up with several police cars and got their attention. The gang members exited the freeway and were gone.

The gangs felt empowered after the riot. They had the police on the run, and the community was petrified. It took many months to restore order.

All of our construction, maintenance, service, and computer department personnel were busy preparing our locations to reopen for business. We brought trailers onto the parking lots of the two branches that had been burned, and all our locations were back open for business within a week.

We paid Western Union the $5 million we owed them. I told Pam she'd been right not to trust the city's promises, and said I would never make that mistake again. Our insurance brokers, Sheldon and Andrea Shapiro, started working on our insurance claim. We had a "We Survived the Riot" celebration dinner with all of our people, and gave special recognition to our security team and the volunteers who kept us safe.

Shortly after the riot, we were approached by Reverend Romie Lily, who worked with The Southern Area Clergy Council. Together, we developed a "Stop the Violence" campaign, which involved developing anti-gang programs and a billboard campaign to spread the message of how gang warfare affected individuals, families, and communities. Reverend Lily was honored by the Carter Center for his work. Romie and I became good friends, and we continued to work together to combat other issues affecting the community, such as domestic violence.

We received considerable publicity and goodwill thanks to our efforts. We also got a surge of new business on account of the fact that many of our competitors had been burned down. However, we were struggling with all of the cost and loss of cash as a result of the riot, and it took a year of back-and-forth with our insurance company before we received a $2 million check to settle our claim.

We were finally on solid ground financially and ready to take the next step with our business.

News footage of Nix Check Cashing during the 1992 riot can be viewed at **www.nixland.net**.

CHAPTER 8

Store-within-Store

In 1993, we had an opportunity to prove our corporate culture of being an "event-driven business." J.J. Newberry's was a five-and-dime store chain, with hundreds of stores across the country. We opened a "store-within-store" in their Compton location on Rosecrans and Central, so customers shopping at J.J. Newberry's could also get their checks cashed by Nix Check Cashing. It was a good opportunity for us and for our customers.

A couple weeks after we opened, we got a visit from the store's famous owner, Meshulam Riklis. Riklis owned dozens of companies, was married to singer Pia Isadora, and was frequently in the news. We were excited to meet him. Dave Robinson and I showed him our modular 12' x 12' booth, which Dave had designed. This booth had three check-cashing windows and could be installed in a matter of days. I gave Riklis a demonstration of our point-of-sale computer system, and talked about our strategy of providing fast, friendly, courteous service, at a fair and reasonable price, from locations that were clean, well-maintained, and professionally staffed with people who lived right in the neighborhood.

Riklis loved it! He said in a loud, excited voice, "This is like the pussy and the dick." He explained: "The check-cashing booth is like a pussy, and the rest of the store is like a dick. They'll come for the pussy, and then they'll get the dick."

Then he said to me, "I want to buy a hundred franchise stores." He shook my hand vigorously and rushed off.

Dave and I looked at each other and said, "What the fuck just happened?" We were flabbergasted! We didn't have any kind of franchise program, but we would surely develop one. A few months later, we signed a franchise agreement with Riklis for a hundred stores.

This was our new business strategy. We would open company-owned "store-within-stores" (SWS) and sell SWS franchises directly to retail chains, as well as franchises to standalone check-cashing store operators. The SWS strategy would allow us to expand our company-owned network at a fraction of the cost of opening our much-larger 1500 ft. to 2000 ft. locations. This meant our initial capital outlay per store was less, so we'd hit our breakeven point sooner and profitability much more quickly.

We were fortunate to have gotten good press and TV coverage for many years, along with our ongoing radio, TV advertising, and community outreach programs, all of which helped establish our credibility with retailers.

To take advantage of this opportunity in a meaningful way, we needed to raise capital. Our existing organization was separated into numerous limited partnerships, but for this venture, we needed one corporation that owned all of the assets of the company. This would streamline our operations by eliminating the need to keep distinct accounting records for all of the separate entities. More importantly, it would bring us closer to our ultimate goal: we wanted to go public, or sell our business to a strategic buyer.

By the end of 1993, we were successful in rolling up the different parts of our business into one corporation. We offered our investors a tax-free exchange of their limited partnership interest for stock in the new corporation. Every investor except one voted for the rollup. The rollup allowed us to get a sizable line of credit with Wells Fargo Bank. I also sold $2.3 million in five-year convertible subordinated notes that paid 10 percent annual return to our investor base.

In 1995, the Food 4 Less supermarket chain contacted us about taking over a check-cashing booth in their Watts store on 103rd Street and Compton Avenue. Founders Bank, an African-American owned institution, was operating the check-cashing business in the market with very little success. They wanted out and Food 4 Less wanted to replace them with an organization that had an excellent reputation in the community. We jumped on the opportunity.

Food 4 Less was a new concept in the grocery business. They ran large warehouse-type stores where customers bagged their own groceries and were not provided the service of cashing government or payroll checks. Having an independent third party provide check-cashing services was a perfect fit. However, Food 4 Less was worried about the reputation risk of having a check casher tarnish their reputation. They were not concerned about this problem with Nix Check Cashing.

Within a short time, we had quadrupled the volume that Founders Bank was doing, which resulted in increased grocery sales for Food 4 Less. We brought in customers with cash to spend! Our strong brand name and outstanding customer service was fueling the business, and our three-window check-cashing booth became exceptionally profitable. Our cost of doing business inside of the market was much lower, too. Rent was only a few hundred dollars per month, and we had no need for security to protect the business. It was much safer operating inside the store, which had many other employees working nearby. It also took a lot less capital to set up a store-within-store.

Founders Bank was astonished that we were doing so

well when they hadn't been able to make a go of it. The problem with banks is that they are risk adverse. Banks normally cash a check for a customer who has funds on deposit to cover the check if it is returned, and when the customer does not have sufficient funds on deposit, the bank places a hold on the check until it clears. Check cashers, on the other hand, take a risk on every single check-cashing transaction, and must become good at measuring risk. Taking too few risks hurts revenue, and taking too many risks results in skyrocketing bad check costs. Nix Check Cashing was good at measuring risks.

Food 4 Less wanted us to open more stores inside of their markets, and we were thrilled with the opportunity.

We had passed the litmus test with two retail chains, which would make it easier for us to convince other supermarkets and retailers to let us operate inside their stores. We only offered retailers $400-$500 a month rent, but we could help them increase their store sales as much as 20 percent.

The investment side of Wells Fargo Bank was also interested in making an equity investment in our company. That was great news for us: our SWS program was taking off, and we needed equity capital to fund our growth. We had numerous meetings with the investment side of the Wells Fargo Bank. Our commercial banker, Dave Gonzales, and my entire top management team were convinced that Wells Fargo was going to make an equity investment in our company.

Based on this confidence, we continued to expand our company, using funds from our credit line. The credit line was not designed to be used for this sort of long-term investment, and it was risky, but our commercial banker supported my decision to use it for this purpose temporarily, until permanent capital was in place. We had a great market opportunity to grow our store-within-store program, and I didn't want it to get away from us.

We were breaking the mold for the check-cashing industry by teaming up with well-respected retailers in a manner not previously thought possible. One of our main competitors began following our lead and opening stores inside of major retailers.

During our expansion phase, we grew our chain to eighty-seven stores. We opened SWS locations in Food 4 Less, Ralph's, Thrifty Drug stores (which later became Rite Aid), Hughes Markets, Pic 'N' Save (which later became Big Lots), Safeway's Pac N Save, Foods Co, Cala Foods, Payless Drug, Sav Max, Food Giant, Shell gas stations, and a number of independent markets and retailers. We even opened a SWS inside a McDonald's. We also opened sixteen SWS franchise locations in J.J. Newberry's, prior to them closing all of their California stores and exiting the market.

Our rapid growth had been financed by loans we'd taken out against our credit line, on the belief that Wells Fargo would soon be investing in an equity share of our company. But Wells Fargo's interest came to an abrupt halt when they decided to merge with First Interstate Bank. All of the bank's new investments were put on the back burner until the merger was finished. Since merging these two big banks was a monumental undertaking, we knew that Wells Fargo's investment dollars wouldn't be coming our way anytime soon. We now desperately needed to raise capital, to replace the funds we'd used to expand the business from our credit line.

The mad dash was on! We hired a local investment banker and worked months on our offering circular and sales process, but in the end, we were unable to raise the capital we needed. Wells Fargo got impatient, and transferred our account to the "workout" section of the bank. This is not a good place to be.

We continued meeting with investment bankers and financiers, but they all smelled blood. They wanted to recapitalize the company by taking out my investor base, and me, with no compensation for the ownership of the company. I would get a sweetheart deal with large salary and stock options in the newly restructured company. This was not something I would even consider. It was not the right thing to do.

In desperation, I hired Oppenheimer & Co. to sell the company, and began working with an investment banker named Mike Abrahams. Mike was a great guy and we got along very well. He could see the potential of our company, and he asked me why I wanted to sell. I told him that really, it was the last thing I wanted to do, but the company was on the ropes: we needed the capital to repay Wells Fargo. Mike said he felt he could raise the capital that we needed in a short time, and I jumped at the opportunity.

He called a friend of his named John Lapham, who had just started working for SunAmerica Corporate Finance. He told him he had a rare investment opportunity. John could see our potential immediately. We met with his boss, Jim Hunt, who was the director of the investment division, and he could see it, too.

SunAmerica made a sizable investment in our company within record time. It was a fair deal for them, for my investors, and for me. We were back in growth mode, fueled with capital and a great partner. We were absolutely positive we could reach our goal of going public or being acquired by a strategic partner within five years. John Lapham, Jim Hunt, and I forged a great relationship.

SunAmerica wanted me to bring in a new CFO. Mike Abrahams recommended a friend of his, Randy Dotemoto, for the CFO position. Randy was a CPA who'd had a long career with one of the big accounting firms, Arthur Anderson. Randy was a fabulous addition to our team, and we hit it off really well. Randy, Darline, and I each had our strengths and weaknesses, but we complemented each other and became what we referred to as a three-legged stool.

Our relationship with Wells Fargo was so strained, we needed to get a new bank to service our business. I called the Vice Chairman of Union Bank of California, Rick Hartnack. I first met Rick in 1992, when he told me his bank was interested in getting into the check-cashing business. He said he'd asked around and heard we were the best check-cashing company there was. He wanted to hire us as a consultant to teach the bank the business.

I wanted to do it in the worst way, especially after making over $1 million in consulting fees with Western Union in 1990-91. But I didn't feel right about offering our services for a fee after just kicking off Wunix. I felt it would be bad for my relationship with Western Union. We were launching what we thought would become the first nationwide check-cashing company, and I didn't think they would have looked fondly on me helping a large company become our competitor. Personally, though, I was excited to see a well-respected bank get into the check-cashing business and help improve our industry's reputation.

Our industry was beginning to come of age. The

consumer protection legislation I had recently spearheaded had eliminated most of the unscrupulous operators, and competition had forced others to improve their service.

I told Rick he was welcome to tour our business and I would openly share our procedures with him at no charge. He took me up on it, and I met with him and his people several times. We developed a good relationship.

Rick launched one of the country's first bank-owned check-cashing companies, and called it Cash & Save. They opened locations inside some of their bank branches, inside of grocery stores, and had one standalone location. He wanted to provide customers who lived in low- to moderate-income communities the option of check cashing across the lobby from their traditional teller line. He could send customers who routinely came to cash checks at the banking windows across the lobby to cash their check at Cash & Save instead of sending them out the door. He could also transition check-cashing customers who were moving up the financial ladder to traditional banking services. It was the same strategy we had with Western Union through our Wunix joint venture.

Rick invited Randy and me to his office in downtown Los Angeles to meet with him and one of his commercial bankers, Chuck Amico. Chuck was different than most bankers, because he was willing to think outside of the box and had an entrepreneurial spirit. By the time we left the meeting, we had a new bank, and I would become lifetime friends with Rick and Chuck. It's critical for a check-cashing business to have a strong relationship with a bank, because the bank has to process millions of dollars in cash and checks each week. Now we had a fabulous new bank, and a $6 million equity investment from SunAmerica. We were back on track!

By the end of 1997, our business was progressing nicely. We had expanded the company from twenty-five branches in 1993 to eighty-seven branches. We lost money for much of this expansion period, because each new branch loses money in the beginning. Check cashing is a service business, and, unlike retail, you cannot run a grand opening celebration to spike sales or create more demand. People only get one check per pay period, so demand is fixed. Everyone near the new branch is cashing their checks somewhere already, typically at another check casher, market, liquor store, or bank. This means you have to wean customers off their existing provider by inspiring them to your store. You can have low introductory pricing, a location that has high visibility, easy access, plenty of parking, and better service than your competitors, thereby creating strong word-of-mouth advertising. Our strong brand name, a large pool of card-carrying customers, and the convenience of cashing checks at our "store-within-store" locations, at a retailer customers regularly visited, also helped encourage people to leave their current provider and try Nix Check Cashing.

We had originally projected that our new stores would hit breakeven in twelve months, but in reality, we were experiencing about an eighteen-month breakeven point. This is still a relatively short time in the financial service industry. A new bank branch generally takes four to five years to reach breakeven. All we had to do to become a very profitable company was to stop growing.

Our plan was to grow the company to about a hundred branches, and make sure we had the platform and infrastructure in place to take the company public or get acquired by a strategic partner. We had invested in upgrading our point-of-sale computer system, doubled the size of our main office, and beefed up our management team. We expected to be ready to go to market by the end of 1998. It was an exciting time. We had been through so many challenges in the past five years, and had overcome all of them. Phenomenal success was just around the corner.

I was surprised one day in November 1997 to receive a call from John Lapham, telling me he and Jim Hunt wanted to meet at their office in the SunAmerica building in Century City. This was highly unusual. The only time we saw John was at our monthly board meeting, which was held at our office in Carson, and we rarely saw Jim. It was a worrisome call.

A few days later, we met. Jim took the lead and told us

that SunAmerica was going to be acquired by AIG. American International Group was a huge insurance company, and had at one time been our insurance carrier. He went on to explain that they were refocusing the mission of SunAmerica Corporate Finance, and were pulling out of small investments like ours. He said they were also concerned because we had missed our financial targets, and profitability was taking longer than we had expected.

I agreed with him, but told him it was easy to see we were on the verge of turning the corner, and would be very profitable soon. We would be ready to go to market in a year or two. He said they didn't want to wait. They had arranged for a top-flight investment banking group to represent our company and sell us now.

I was sick to my stomach and literally ready to throw up. I went into sales mode, and gave Jim and John my best pitch for why we should wait a couple more years as we had planned. We had agreed to a five-year horizon to have an exit for SunAmerica, but we had only been partners for year and a half. But they could not be convinced.

Jim then pulled his trump card. He reminded me of my promise to him. Prior to closing our deal with SunAmerica in May of 1996, I told Jim and John that investing with us was zero risk. I told them that our company had enough intrinsic value that we could always sell it for enough money to repay their investment. In that conversation, I promised to sell the company if we didn't perform as expected. Back then, I was desperate to bring in capital, and thrilled at the opportunity of partnering with SunAmerica. Looking back, I realize they probably would have invested without me making that promise. But I did make it, and now I was stuck with it. I live by the adage, "A man's word is his worth." I had no option but to agree to sell the company. Jim thanked me for supporting his decision, and we all shook hands.

I was crushed. Darline and Randy felt the same way. We had worked night and day for the past five years to achieve our mission, and we were so close. I kept asking myself, "Why did I make that promise?" Dad always said, "It's okay to feel sorry for yourself and pout once in a while, but give yourself a deadline, and when you reach that deadline, kick yourself in the ass, put it behind you, and start moving forward." This is very good advice, but it takes strong discipline to do it when it's something that changes your whole life. It took me longer than usual to adjust to this adversity.

To make matters worse, Randy and Mike Abrahams were advising me not to sell. They felt they could easily raise the capital to take SunAmerica out. Darline didn't want to sell, either. It was clear to see that our business was ready to become profitable, and selling it in a year or two would bring us a much better price. We were crippled, short-term, by three years of losses on our balance sheet, and the buzzards would be circling.

I tried to rationalize my thinking in a way that would let me break my promise. I couldn't do it. I had no option but to sell. I kicked myself in the ass, stopped feeling sorry for myself, and started moving forward.

We decided to go with the investment banking firm SunAmerica had recommended, and signed an engagement contract with them in early 1998. We felt we would have never been able to attract a high-profile company like that if it were not for SunAmerica, so we might as well take advantage of it.

By June of 1998, we had a deal to sell the company. It was an okay deal under the circumstances. I was pleased we had the time to write and sign a definitive agreement before September. This was important, because our $2.3 million worth of five-year convertible subordinated notes were due in September. The buyer agreed to close the transaction prior to the notes expiring so I could pay that obligation on time.

That didn't happen. I was now in default and beside myself. I wrote a letter to my note holders telling them the circumstances and pledging to pay them as soon as possible. We expected the deal to close any day. Instead, the buyer dragged out the legal process for weeks by throwing up detail after detail. He was obviously stalling.

I knew we were being set up for the kill. The buyer was taking advantage of our situation with our note holders and SunAmerica's anxiousness to get out of the deal. I needed another way out of this mess.

I decided to contact Jeff Silverman, one of our major competitors and owner of USA Check Cashing. Jeff was also one of the founders of the National Check Cashers Association, and we had worked together on association business and political matters in California. We had butted heads on many occasions over the years, but we had a cordial relationship. I told Jeff my situation and that I would give him a sweetheart deal for our Northern California stores if he was interested in purchasing them. He jumped at the opportunity and agreed to be my backup.

I met with Lapham and told him about Jeff. We now had a safety valve if the buyer backed out. The sale of our twenty-four Northern California stores and two of our Southern California stores would give us the cash we needed to pay off the notes, plus some additional cash for the business. However, it would not provide an exit for SunAmerica.

I told John I wanted to have an all-hands meeting to work out the remaining details of the sales contract with our buyer, and if we could not finalize the deal, then I would sell the stores to USA Check Cashing so I could pay off the notes. We set up the meeting for a week later. It was December 1998.

I left my home in Fountain Valley about 5:30 a.m. on the morning of the meeting. The meeting was scheduled for 9 a.m. at an office near Century City. It could take me hours in rush-hour traffic to get there, so I planned on getting there early, to eat a high-protein breakfast, then meditate in my car. I wanted to be on my toes for our final meeting to close the deal.

About forty-five minutes before the meeting, I got a call from a representative at SunAmerica and was told, "We want you to take the deal this morning." I said, "What do you mean?" The representative said, "The buyer is changing his offer, and we want you to take the deal." Then he hung up.

I met Randy, our longtime trusted attorney Bernie Shearer, and his associate, Mike Bales, in the lobby of the building. I told them the buyer was changing his offer, and I wanted them to wait there until I went in to see what was going on. I walked into the conference room, and there sat the buyer, his attorney, the SunAmerica representative, and our broker.

I took a seat across the table from the four of them and said, "What's going on?" The buyer said he had reconsidered his offer and had decided to reduce it by 25 percent. This was the setup I was worried about, and the fact that my partners and my broker were apprised of the situation before me was outrageous. I said "Let me think about it," and walked out.

We had worked on this deal for six months, and the fact that our broker had not called us prior to the meeting to inform us of the change was despicable. We could see we had clearly made a mistake going with the broker SunAmerica had recommended. We, in fact, were not the client, even though we signed the engagement agreement and paid all the bills. We should have gone with our own broker.

I asked Bernie to explain our options. He said, "You don't really have any. If you don't sell the company, SunAmerica will take you to court, and take it from you. You have not performed financially as you were required to do under your agreement with them, so they have the right to take over the company and you have no defense. You will end up with nothing if you don't sell it."

I left Bernie's office and drove to my sailboat. I spent all afternoon sitting on the boat, thinking. I felt SunAmerica and our broker had sold us out. I felt I no longer had any moral obligation to them. They had let me off the hook with their behavior. It was now merely a personal decision. If I took the deal, my investors and I would get about $2.25 per share. The average purchase price for our investors was about $7.50 per share. It was a crappy deal. (Nine years later we sold for $18 a share after paying $.50 per share in dividends for a number of years.) On the other hand, $2.25 was better than a complete loss. I owned a big chunk of the company, and would get about $2 million if

I agreed to the sale. Part of the agreement was for me to work in the buyer's company, but now that was out of the question. I would not work with someone who had absolutely no sense of fair play. But selling the company was a difficult decision, and I stewed on it all day.

I went home that evening and explained the whole situation to Pam. I asked her what she thought we should do. She said, "Tom, what do you want to do"? I told her I didn't want to sell it. We would be forgoing $2 million, which was a huge amount of money to us, and that we would probably lose our home. She said, "Fine and I'm with you 100 percent. We have each other, and we can start over. We can rent an apartment, and you can get another job, and I will go back to work, too." I was so grateful for her support.

The next morning, I called Darline and Randy and told them my decision. They were ecstatic. I then called SunAmerica and told them I was not going to do the deal. Instead, I was going to sell our Northern California stores to USA Check Cashing and pay off the notes. I told SunAmerica I would focus the company on making money, instead of growing, and that I would do my best to find a new partner to take them out of the investment as soon as I could.

SunAmerica threatened to sue us, and I threatened to countersue because of their behavior. I promised to protest

their unfair treatment of us by busing hundreds of my customers to picket around the SunAmerica building, pass
out a hundred thousand flyers to our customers revealing
that they were putting Nix Check Cashing out of business, and mount a public relations campaign to make sure
everyone in the business community found out about their
actions. I ended my statements by saying that I was well
aware that they would win in court, but they would get
bloodied in the process. I was in a street fight, and ready to
kick, bite, or do whatever was necessary to survive. SunA-
merica had seen me in action and they knew I was not
making idle threats.

I said, "The alternative is for you to support my decision, and give me time to find a partner to replace you."

It just so happened that we had a pre-scheduled board
meeting for the next day. My loyal friend and long-time
board member Bob Best said, "How many times do you
think this 'I am going to fall on my sword' threat of yours
is going to work before you actually have to do it"? I said,
"Just one more time is all I need."

Fortunately for everyone, SunAmerica decided to give
us the time we needed to find a way to buy them out. They
gave us 100 percent support from that day forward.

We made drastic changes in January 1999. We had our
first and only layoff in the forty-two years we'd owned the
company. We laid off twenty-four employees, mostly from

our corporate headquarters. It was a very difficult decision for me to lay off part of my team, but it had to be done. We did it in the most sympathetic way we could, and provided everyone with a severance package. We had twenty-six fewer stores to support, and reduced our work force from about 650 employees to about 450 as result of the sale of Gold Star Check Cashing. Plus, we were not going to grow the chain. We sold our Security Products Division to one of our salesmen, and we had already stopped selling franchises the year before. We reduced the size of our main office. We had one goal: MAKE PROFIT!

We had a scheduled companywide meeting for our managers, and the night before the meeting, I was on my sailboat, thinking about how to pull the team together, when Bob Seger's song, "Like A Rock," started playing in the background. That was it! The song talked about a man who used to be like a rock, but had gotten off track, and needed to see himself as a rock again. It was a perfect analogy for our company.

I gave an enthusiastic speech about how we had grown too fast and spread ourselves too thin. This had allowed us to forget that we are all one team. I knew if we could come together, we would be very profitable and very successful. I played them the Bob Seger song, and said, "From now on, we're going to be one team, like a rock."

It all worked. We were profitable that year and every

year thereafter. A few years later, we began paying dividends to our shareholders, which we had not done since the rollup in 1993. Our investor group, with very few exceptions, stood by us with no complaints during this entire period. They knew we were giving it our best, and cheered us on with their fingers crossed. I'm grateful for their support during those lean and challenging years.

CHAPTER 9

Union Bank of California

Mike Abrahams and Randy spent the first six months of 1999 looking for a replacement for SunAmerica. They talked to dozens of firms, and we did a few tours of our business, but they could not find an interested party. It was very discouraging.

One night that summer, I was sitting in the cockpit of my sailboat, listening to music, drinking a beer, and thinking about our predicament when I thought of the solution. I got very excited!

The next morning, I called Rick Hartnack, my friend from Union Bank, and told him we needed to team up. It was a perfect fit. Union Bank had its Cash & Save check-cashing stores and wanted to penetrate the underserved market, but had almost no branches in the inner city. We had branches throughout the inner city but didn't have banking services. We could both accomplish our missions better if we teamed up.

Rick agreed: it was a natural fit.

We met at 6 a.m. at the Norms Restaurant on Pacific Coast Highway in Torrance a few days later. We hit it off. The strategy was indeed perfect, and Rick and I bonded very well. He was a fighter pilot in Vietnam flying over 200 combat missions. I had spent ten years as a Reserve Deputy Sheriff in the heart of the inner city. We were both fighters. We also seemed to have a similar outlook towards management and leadership. We were both stand-up guys. We could team up and change the world.

We outlined the deal on the back of a few napkins and shook on it. He warned me, "Remember, it is not the bank of Rick." He needed to get board approval, but felt it would be no problem.

A few weeks later, he called me and said the board did not approve the plan. I told him I understood. Then I went on to give the sales pitch of my life. I reminded him of all the reasons that we should be partners: it was the opportunity of a lifetime. When I finally stopped talking, he said, "You're right, Tom. We can't pass this up. I've got to try harder to convince the board."

Two weeks later, he called me and said we have a deal. I was euphoric!

In March of 2000, we took the deal to SunAmerica,

and John Lapham and Jim Hunt were very pleased. They thought about it overnight and took the deal as it was presented. They could've haggled over parts of the offer, but didn't. I appreciated that very much. It turned out to be a good investment for SunAmerica, returning them about 25 percent annually, but it was not the homerun we'd all hoped for.

Nevertheless, it was time to celebrate. SunAmerica was happy to be out of the Nix investment, and Nix and Union Bank were excited to be teaming up to change the way financial services were delivered to low- and moderate-income communities.

Working with Rick Hartnack and Union Bank was the best experience of my career. Hartnack was a fabulous leader, with the awesome ability to inspire everyone who worked with him to do his or her very best. The best definition of leadership I know of is "the ability to inspire the willing cooperation of others towards the accomplishment of common goals," and Rick could do it better than anyone I had ever met. The majority of the bank's 10,000 employees reported through Hartnack's chain of command, and he was admired throughout the bank.

He was also a visionary and a risk-taker who was totally committed to bringing banking back to underserved communities. He knew the standard bank approach had proven unprofitable in these communities, but he believed that combining traditional banking with alternative financial services such as check cashing could create the low-cost distribution system necessary to make it work. The combination of Union Bank and Nix Check Cashing would allow people to transition into banking as they moved up the financial ladder. We could accomplish what our alliance partner John Bryant always talked about: "doing well by doing good." That is exactly what we were doing. We believed we were going to change the world.

Union Bank was 100 percent committed to creating diversity in the workplace, and was chosen as the best company in the country for minorities by Fortune in 1999. Rick geared up about half a dozen Union Bank people, all minorities, to work directly with us under the command of Thom Branch. Thom was an excellent fit: a smart, savvy, well-educated black man who had passion for our mission. We also coordinated with Yolanda Brown, a sharp black woman who was senior vice president and division manager of Union Bank's Cash & Save division. It was no accident that minority folks were chosen to help us change the world for underserved communities across our nation. We not only had the talent to get it done, we had the passion. And it was a perfect fit for Nix Check Cashing, with over 90 percent of its workforce made up of minority people.

John Bryant, president and CEO of Operation Hope, was another important ingredient needed to change the world. His organization promoted a program called "Banking on the Future," which taught people how to properly manage a bank account. He did not like the check-cashing industry, but he felt differently about Nix Check Cashing and me, and he could see the magic we were creating. John was very influential politically, and he helped politicians and regulators—people who wanted to do good things for the underserved communities—to see the genius in our business model.

We referred to our team as the "Union Bank of Nix." We focused everyone on the task of figuring out how to add Union Bank services to our branches. This was a monumental undertaking, made more difficult by the bank's regulatory environment. We ultimately developed a system that would allow customers to open a Union Bank account at Nix, and then use the Union Bank ATM at each location to conduct their banking. It was a hybrid model that was not true over-the-counter banking, but that would have to wait until Union Bank purchased our company and made it a division of the bank.

We developed an incredible advertising and marketing campaign with our fabulous director of marketing, Tracy Fairbanks, and the help of Union Bank's marketing department. It included radio, cable TV, billboards, direct mail, and expertly produced vignettes that played on a flat-screen TV above the teller windows, encouraging

Nix customers to open a Union Bank account. Union Bank also sent a letter to their business customers, telling them about our alliance.

It was working! In our best year, we signed up about 4,000 new accounts with about one million ATM transactions at the thirty-six Nix locations that offered Union Bank products and services.

As the partnership grew, we discovered the three-window store-within-store locations that we had worked so hard to get in place were just too small to add full-service banking. We decided to relocate them to larger, standalone locations. This was a huge task, and required us to find a location very close by, to be able to move the customers to the new location. Customers cash their checks where they live or work, and are not willing to drive out of their way. A badly planned relocation might drive our customers to a competitor. But with careful planning, we successfully relocated most of our store-within-store locations within a couple of years.

Hartnack asked me not to open any more locations until after Union Bank acquired our company. He said, "I don't want to be supporting the growth of your network if it will just cost me more money to buy you in a couple of years." I had no trouble agreeing to his request. Hartnack saved our company from the wolves with his courage and tenacity, and he was spending a sizable amount of money in labor and other expenses to create a successful business model. I owed Hartnack, and was anxious to support him in any way I could. Besides, Union Bank planned to begin an aggressive acquisition plan as soon as we became a division of the bank. This would allow us to create a large branch network in relatively short order. I was so excited to see my dream coming true and all of the adventure that it would bring. I expected to be Union Bank's division president.

We had an ongoing problem with our "payday product." A payday loan is actually a very good product when used correctly, but it is misunderstood by those who have never had a reason to use it. It is a quick, easy, and dignified transaction. The consumer writes a personal check, post-dated until their next payday, and leaves our store with up to $300, less the fee. Back in the days of the Mini Mart, my dad and I would regularly take a post-dated check from a customer when they needed food and couldn't immediately cover the expense. This way, we made a grocery sale that we otherwise would have lost, and it gave us a happy customer.

The payday transaction at Nix was very similar. We charged a larger fee than we would for a basic check cashing, because we were deferring the deposit of the check until the customer had the money. We filled a need, provided a service, and made a happy customer.

What does a person do when they have an urgent need

for a little extra cash to pay for food, medicine, gas, a car repair to get to work, a utility bill to keep the lights on, or any of the broad array of life's little cash crunches? Banks don't lend small amounts of money because there's not enough profit. People might draw from their savings, or borrow from their credit card or from a friend. But if they don't have these options, then their choices aren't very good. They can bounce a check, pay a bill late, go to a pawn shop, do something illegal, or take out a payday loan.

Payday loans generally cost less than a bounced check fee or the penalty on a late bill, and the service is not demeaning like using a pawn shop. This is why the product is so popular. Consumers are smart enough to figure out which option costs them less, and they choose it.

There's a misconception that only poor people use payday loans. In reality, most people who use the payday product are middle-income or above. This is why you see many payday locations in middle- and upper-middle-income communities. Understand, a person must have a checking account to get a payday loan, and most poor people are unbanked. The relatively small percentage of bank customers in low-income communities is the reason that only about 20 percent of Nix revenue came from payday loans.

The major problem with the payday product is that it can be easily misused by people who get loan after loan. I lobbied very hard at the state legislature to create a law that would have required payday lenders to give a payday customer ninety days to pay off their payday loan after they had four loans in a row. My actions infuriated the payday loan industry. They couldn't understand how I could team up with consumer groups in a way that would damage their business. I felt if we could eliminate the problematic nature of the product, we could legitimize it, and ensure it would pass the test of time. We did manage to pass some additional regulations on payday loans, but not my mandatory 90-day payoff plan.

I asked Hartnack if we could create a 90-day loan at Union Bank that we could offer to our customers. This new type of loan would allow payday loan customers who were caught in the cycle of debt to find a more affordable way to start working their way out. It would be great for our customers and would attract new customers from our payday loan competitors.

Hartnack thought it was a good idea, and teamed us with the proper people in the bank. The credit people didn't like the loan, but if that was what Hartnack wanted, they would do their best. Nix Check Cashing agreed to assume the bad debt created by the product, so the bank was not at risk.

We developed a terrific product that was about half the cost of a payday loan, rolled over each pay period for ninety days.

The program was a disaster! People basically said to themselves, "Great! Free money!" and never paid us back. Nix Check Cashing lost 80 percent of the money we loaned with this product. It was a huge disappointment, after working months to develop it in accordance with all of the compliance issues. I called Hartnack one day and said, "The 90-day loan looks like a bust. What do you think we should do?" He said, "It's your product, Tom, and I will support whatever decision you make." I decided to wind it down.

This experience taught me the value of collateral. The personal check in the payday loan transaction is a form of collateral. The customer is inspired to repay the payday loan, because otherwise the post-dated check will be deposited, resulting in an overdraft charge and possibly even the loss of their bank account. The 90-day loan didn't work, but I decided I would continue to look for ways to make payday loans a better product.

Meanwhile, though, the partnership between Union Bank and Nix Check Cashing was bringing banking back to underserved communities. We were creating a phenomenal new business model, and the entire Nix organization and "Union Bank of Nix" was fired up. We had a streamlined form of banking in place at thirty-six locations by 2004, and we would be able to create full-service, over-the-counter banking as soon as we were acquired by Union Bank.

In March of 2004, we were all excited to open a new Union Bank branch with a Nix Check Cashing and an Operation Hope in the same building. We were 100 percent inspired to launch this new business model. This new hybrid branch would change the world for underserved communities.

I was having a great adventure, and was part of a special team of people who were creating a truly revolutionary business approach. And we were having fun in the process. I flew with Hartnack in his private plane, he and his wife sailed on our boat, we toured Greater Los Angeles in a L.A. County Sheriff's helicopter, we participated in the closing ceremony of the New York Stock Exchange complete with personal tour. Thom Branch took Pam and me to a couple of jazz clubs in Harlem. I spoke with dozens of legislators in Washington, D.C. and Sacramento about our program, and had an opportunity to briefly meet President George W. Bush. I gave a speech to hundreds of people at the L.A. inner-city economic summit just prior to Vice President Al Gore's speech, and as a result, I later received a VIP tour of the White House, including a view of the Oval Office and the Situation Room. I was proud to have Nix Check Cashing prominently featured in Union Bank's new employee orientation video. We were becoming part of the fabric of Union Bank, and would undoubtedly be a division of the bank soon. Or so we thought.

Unfortunately, we were dealt a devastating blow in March of 2004. The Office of the Comptroller of Currency (OCC) refused to grant permission for Union Bank to purchase Nix Check Cashing.

The OCC was responding to pressure from various well-intentioned but poorly informed consumer groups who were completely opposed to check-cashing institutions. These groups lobbied relentlessly against alternative banking, in the hope that somehow traditional banks would return to the same low-income communities they'd left decades ago.

But banks cannot make money with the traditional banking model in these communities. It is economically unfeasible. Banks are not going to come back to these communities until there is a good business model. This is exactly what Union Bank and Nix Check Cashing would have provided. Our venture would have filled important needs within these communities in a fair manner and at affordable prices. We had a solution to bring full-service, over-the-counter banking to underserved communities. We would have had forty-seven full-service bank branches by the end of 2004, and we had an acquisition strategy that would've added hundreds more. Our competitors would've copied our successful model, and underserved communities all over the country would have benefited from it.

What the consumer groups don't realize is that traditional banking is not for everyone. There are plenty of straightforward reasons some people prefer a simple cash-and-carry approach that does not require balancing a bank statement every month. People who live paycheck to paycheck cannot wait a week to receive their money while banks put a hold on their checks. There is also a sizable percentage of people living in low-income communities who are listed on ChexSystems because of past bank problems, who are ineligible to get a bank account. The ones who have bank accounts learn quickly that the cost of a few bounced checks can quickly exceed the cost of using a check casher.

Plus, banks do not offer all of the services used by low-income people, such as inexpensive money orders, money transfer, bus passes, DMV registration services, fax services, and prepaid mobile phone cards. These services, along with check cashing and payday loans, would have created a platform for banks to be profitable on a lower-volume scale, so they could provide traditional banking services to those consumers that could use it.

The OCC's decision ensured that no bank would ever duplicate the experience Union Bank had with Nix Check Cashing, and made it harder for people in these communities to access traditional banking services and begin moving up the financial ladder. It was a crying shame! We could have changed America, and it was terribly disappointing to have been refused the opportunity to do so.

In March of 2005, I received a call from Hartnack. He said, "I have bad news, I'm leaving the bank." I said, "When?" He said, "Today."

We agreed to meet the next morning at Norms on Pacific Coast Highway for breakfast, where he would give me the details. I was literally sick to my stomach. Hartnack and I were planning to take another run at the OCC when the current director left the organization. We hoped the new director would be better grounded in the realities of the marketplace and more courageous.

I knew in my heart that Union Bank would not go forward with our plans without Hartnack. He had the passion, vision, and courage necessary to ultimately prevail, and he truly cared about the underserved community. No one could take his place.

We met the next morning at Norms restaurant, where it all started. He told me he was going to become the vice chairman of US Bank, and maybe somehow we could team up in the future to accomplish the mission. We both knew that was just wishful thinking. We were like two Army generals who had just lost the war, having breakfast talking about what could've been.

Within a few months of Hartnack leaving, Thom Branch and Yolanda Brown both retired, and all of the people at the "Union Bank of Nix" were relocated to new jobs within the bank. We had no direct contact in the bank. I met with the new Vice Chairman, Phil Flynn, over lunch. He told me the bank had retained consultants to help them develop a new strategic plan, and the future of Nix could not be certain until it was completed. He said we could have one of three outcomes: continue the mission as we had originally envisioned it; keep the relationship as it was, with no plans to expand it; or exit the investment.

He said, "Just run your business and continue everything you're doing for Union Bank, and if you need to talk to someone about any issues, call me." I never called him.

We bumped along for many months, and during this period, I exercised our option to repurchase one-half of the bank's ownership in our company, bringing them down to a 20 percent stake.

In August of 2006, I finally got a call from George Ramirez, the Market President for the Los Angeles area. George and I had a good relationship and met for lunch to discuss the future. He said he was now responsible for Nix Check Cashing and would be my point of contact. He said the bank was happy with our relationship as it was, but did not plan on expanding it or acquiring us. They had chosen Option Number Two.

George invited me to the unveiling of their new corporate strategy to be held the following month. The new focus was to shift away from the community banking model Hartnack had engineered, and begin focusing on high net worth individuals and commercial accounts. It had a familiar ring, and I knew there was no place for Nix Check Cashing in the long run. I talked to Pam and my sons Bill and Tom and they all agreed. Darline, Randy, and I decided we would put the company up for sale.

Video vignettes played in the lobby of Nix Check Cashing locations to inspire consumers to open a Union Bank account can be viewed at **www.nixland.net**.

CHAPTER 10

Kinecta Federal Credit Union

Our mission was to get acquired by the highest bidder, but if possible, we wanted a strategic buyer who would allow us to capitalize on the value of our network, create career opportunities for our employees, and continue to fill important needs in the community. We were a highly unique company in the check-cashing industry, and I wanted to capitalize on this fact, rather than merely selling out to one of our competitors. However, balancing these competing goals proved to be quite a challenge during the process. Oftentimes, the highest bidder is not always the best fit culturally for the company, and conversely, sometimes the buyer with the best fit culturally does not always offer the best price.

We retained the investment banking firm Barrington Associates in February 2007. Barrington was a wholly owned subsidiary of Wells Fargo Bank. Leading the deal for Barrington was Dave Iannini, a Managing Director who had a lot of experience executing deals for financial service companies. Among many others, Dave counted Bank of America and Wells Fargo as past clients of his. He was also previously the Treasurer of Viad Corp., which owned MoneyGram, the second largest money transfer company in the country. Dave was familiar with the check-cashing industry, and felt he could successfully represent us. Matt Dawson and Don McGreal were assisting him with our project.

Randy and I got along well with Dave and his team. Like many investment bankers, Dave is very aggressive and direct. As Dave explained to me, in the investment banking business, where your fee is completely dependent on closing a deal, you can't pull any punches. We had these traits in common, and I felt he was just the kind of hard-nosed guy we needed to get the job done. I knew we would have lively arguments as the process unfolded, but then again, I enjoyed a good fight, and was looking forward to it.

I wrote the following confidential affirmation in March 2007, shortly after signing the engagement contract with Barrington. I said this affirmation to myself at least a dozen times a day until the day we officially finalized the sale of our company: "We sold Nix Check Cashing by July 31, 2007 to a strategic buyer for over $40 million, to the benefit of our shareholders, employees, and the community."

The process that resulted in the sale of the company to Kinecta was amazing. The Nix and Barrington team worked seven days a week in March and most of April creating the offering memorandum. This was the primary sales tool used to present the company and was about a hundred pages long.

Our marketing strategy was to approach a wide number of interested parties, from private equity firms to strategic buyers. The private equity firms included businesses that might view Nix as a platform for an entry into the alternative financial services business, or those firms that already had an investment in the industry. Strategic buyers included banks, thrifts, and credit unions. We ultimately distributed about seventy-five memoranda to interested parties.

Our objective was to achieve the highest price with the best fit. With this in mind, Iannini counseled us on his approach to first pursue the buyers who would meet the "fit" objective. His view was that, in the end, we could always just sell the company at the highest price to one of our direct check-cashing competitors in a "last-ditch" auction. This way, no "fit" would be required, because the buyer would just fold Nix operations into their own operation, but the Nix name and franchise would be gone forever. I wanted to avoid this scenario, if at all possible.

As a result, our initial efforts were with local private equity firms that viewed Nix Check Cashing as a platform. This way, we could preserve the Nix franchise post-deal. We had many interested buyers, and among those, a Hispanic-market targeted bank that was still in the process of their formation. However, the initial valuations from them and the other buyers were quite low; the "fit" was better, but the price was not. So then we placed our marketing efforts on strategic buyers, mostly financial institutions.

However, most of the institutions ended up not being interested (mainly due to the regulatory concerns we encountered in our dealings with Union Bank). Iannini contacted our direct competitors, but kept them on a "slow track" in order to buy us some more time as we continued to work at finding a more acceptable alternative for a buyer. He was still concerned with the low valuations our competitors were initially discussing with us. With no other adequate bids on the table, and in a bold move to send a message to the market, Dave removed one of the competitors out of the process. As a result, our competitors immediately increased their price indications by $10 million! Even still, Dave kept them on the slow track, because he knew that I wanted more banks and other financial institutions considering our deal. I really wanted to avoid selling to a check-cashing competitor at all costs.

Operation Hope founder and CEO, John Bryant, and I had become friends through the alliance we created with Union Bank. Every year, John Bryant would have a banker's bus tour through South Central Los Angeles in an effort to inspire banks to invest in the low-income community. He always invited me to attend, but I didn't really see any need to go until now. I thought by going on his bank tour this year, I could meet some bankers who might be interested in our company. Iannini cautioned me that it would likely be a complete waste of time as high-level bankers rarely attend such events.

The banker's bus tour started in the rear parking lot of the shopping center located at La Brea Avenue and Rodeo Road. I was surprised to see eight large buses parked along the street just outside the parking lot, and a large tent with the stage. It was not the intimate one or two busloads of high-level bankers I expected. By the time John Bryant started his presentation, there were hundreds of people seated and standing, and most were not from the banking industry. It was clear that Iannini was right—there were not as many high-level bankers there as I thought, and it was perhaps not the best use of my time. I wished I could have left after the presentation to avoid a daylong bus tour through a community that I had been part of for forty years, but I knew John Bryant would be offended, so that was out of the question. But I am glad I stayed. Even though I did not meet a high-level banker, like Dave would have wanted, I met someone even better at the event.

As I began making my way to the buses, I ran into Thom Branch, the Union Bank of California Senior VP in charge of the Nix relationship, who had left the bank the year prior. It was great to see him. On our way to the bus, Thom introduced me to a man named Paul Irving, who sat on the Board of Directors of Operation Hope. Little did I know at the time that this was the chance encounter that would result in the sale of Nix Check Cashing to Kinecta.

Paul and I hit it off immediately. Paul was the Co-chairman, Chief Executive, and Managing Partner of Manatt, Phelps, and Phillips. Their firm specialized in providing legal services to the banking industry, savings and loans, and credit unions. Paul knew Rick Hartnack and was familiar with our mission to bringing banking to underserved communities through a business model that would include alternative financial services. He was a big fan. I told Paul we were trying to sell to a bank or strategic partner, but had little interest from the mainstream financial service industry. He volunteered to introduce us to some of his clients.

I was so excited. I knew my affirmation was working and that this was the break we needed. A few days later, Mike Rosenberg, CEO of Barrington Associates, Randy, and I met with Paul Irving at his office. Iannini could not attend, as he was involved in another deal at the time. Paul talked of dozens of banks that he felt might be interested in taking a look at our deal. Many of the banks he mentioned were ones that Barrington had already contacted, and they expressed little interest due to regulatory concerns. However, I was shocked to hear Mike tell him that Barrington was not interested in pursuing a buyer that had to get regulatory approval. Mike said market intelligence indicated that the regulatory process was so involved and lengthy that it would blow our opportunity to sell to the other interested parties. If the regulators did not ultimately approve the transaction, we would end up with no sale. We had already had that same experience when we tried to sell to Union Bank of California.

I was crushed. After all, we had been trying to accomplish this objective for almost two decades. We wanted to be acquired by a buyer who could help bring banking to underserved communities.

At this point, the only interested parties that we had were two of our major check-cashing competitors, and the previously mentioned Hispanic-targeted bank, that was still in its formation stages. In other words, two birds were easily in hand, and one was way, way out in the bushes. Iannini noted that the Hispanic bank met our objectives on "fit"; however, this opportunity was an absolute non-starter. The bank still needed to be formed, gain regulatory approval, raise capital, and the list went on. Given the serious developments still needed with the Hispanic bank, Dave said it would be absolute insanity for us to pursue them, because we could risk losing bids from our two direct competitors, who were getting increasingly impatient.

He told me I was like Don Quixote chasing windmills: I had failed to accomplish this ridiculous strategy with Western Union, I had failed to create an exit with SunAmerica, and I had failed to sell to Union Bank. He said it was time to stop dreaming and get real. He told me if I blew this opportunity to sell, then I would end up just like Don Quixote: a broken, penniless man.

I understood his warning, but it was my company, and I was not giving up on my dream. It looked like my affirmation was not going to work, but I continued to say it every day. Then, on Sunday June 17, 2007, I received an email from Paul Irving, asking me if I would be interested in talking to Kinecta Federal Credit Union. Paul had been talking to Simone Lagomarsino, CEO of Kinecta, because she used to be on the board of Operation Hope.

Simone told him the National Credit Union Administration was encouraging credit unions to begin providing services in low-income communities, and the Kinecta Board of Directors wanted to buy a check-cashing company as a way to penetrate the underserved market. He asked if she knew that Nix Check Cashing was for sale.

She said, "No, but I know all about Nix Check Cashing." She explained that a number of years prior, she'd been the CFO of Hawthorne Savings and Loan, and they'd been interested in buying or investing in Nix Check Cashing prior to the Union Bank deal. She was very excited about the opportunity, and Paul agreed to contact me.

Randy and I met with Simone and Mark Joseph, Kinecta's CFO at the time, on June 21, 2007. The meeting was phenomenal. On June 26, 2007, Simone and three of her key executives came to our office in Carson, and we took a tour of the main office and visited a branch. It was clear to all that this was a perfect fit.

Iannini also knew when he had a live one. He communicated to Paul Irving that Kinecta was late into the process and that we already had two direct competitors of Nix that were waiting to make high bids. Basically, Kinecta needed to bid "high and hard." Iannini also sought assurance that the deal would gain approval from the NCUA (National Credit Union Administration), the regulator of credit unions. Kinecta approached the NCUA and got a verbal green light.

Iannini negotiated with Kinecta for a couple of weeks. He wanted to get the highest price, and firm and acceptable terms before inking a deal with Kinecta and letting go of the other bidders. He kept everybody on a really tight rope. Finally, on July 11 (Dave's birthday!), Kinecta agreed to pay $45 million for Nix Check Cashing, a price far above what I had hoped for. I want to note that Kinecta's purchase of Nix was the first significant acquisition of a check cashier by a credit union. It was thrilling.

Kinecta immediately started due diligence, complete with a fairness report. On July 19, Randy and I flew to Jackson Hole, Wyoming, and made a presentation to the Kinecta board at their annual strategic conference. We signed a definitive agreement on July 31, subject to shareholder approval and lease assignments from the landlords of the Nix locations.

Then, on August 14, 2007, we closed the deal and received the funds. It was done. My affirmation worked, and my dream of selling Nix Check Cashing to a strategic buyer who would share our mission, care for our employees, and fill the banking needs of the underserved communities had come true.

On August 15, 2007, we had a company-wide managers' meeting and introduced Simone and her team. Simone was amazed to see our entire team start the meeting as we always did, by standing and saying three times, "If you act enthusiastic, you'll be enthusiastic," then finishing with a thunderous, "One team, like a rock!" I was proud because it was obvious that the Nix team was a highly inspired, close-knit group of folks. Simone decided to end each meeting throughout Kinecta with everyone saying, "One team, like a rock."

We had a fabulous strategy. We planned to add Kinecta full-service banking to each of the Nix Check Cashing locations, so the people who lived, worked, or went to school near a Nix location had the opportunity to become a credit union member. We planned to give people the freedom to choose the financial services that best fit their needs, in one convenient location. We planned to let people vote with their feet by choosing the alternative financial services offered by Nix or the traditional banking products and services offered by Kinecta. We also hoped to attract people who were already banking at another institution by offering branches that were more conveniently located inside the inner city.

We started the process of integrating Nix into Kinecta. There were a tremendous number of issues, many of them driven by government regulations required by the NCUA. Simone, Randy, Darline, and I worked hand-in-hand to try and make the necessary changes to Nix with as little disruption as possible. Everyone associated with the integration worked extremely hard to make it happen in a positive way.

Within a few months, all of the people working at the Nix main office in Carson were relocated to Kinecta's main office in Manhattan Beach. Most of the 450 Nix employees got a raise in pay, and all got a better benefit package than we'd had at Nix. I felt we'd teamed up with the very best strategic partner possible.

I know it is customary for business owners to move on within a short while after they sell their business. I thought it would be different for me. I was passionate about our strategy of bringing banking back to underserved communities and to creating career opportunities for the Nix team of people who had been so dedicated to me and the success of Nix Check Cashing. It was not just about me, and I felt obligated to do everything within my power to make things work out well for my former employees, the community, and Kinecta.

I gave it my best as division president for over a year, but it was not working well. I was accustomed to a decentralized approach to managing the business. I did everything within my power for forty years to create the ownership mindset with our entire management team. I gave them each the responsibility and authority to manage their area of the business and held them accountable for their results. We managed by objective and tried to avoid getting involved with the manner and means by which they got things accomplished. We refrained from second-guessing our managers' decisions and looked at their mistakes as learning opportunities. Our mangers were highly motivated and empowered to get excellent results.

We taught and practiced the principles presented in the book *The One Minute Manager* by Kenneth Blanchard.

Kinecta had a centralized form of management that was

in stark contrast to my management style. They believed in Matrix Management and from my point of view got very poor results due to the lack of well-defined responsibility and accountability. There was a lack of respect for the chain of command, and the committee form of management undermined it. There were many other differences including our sense of fair play. I knew Kinecta had purchased the company and could manage it any way they wanted, but it was clear to me that I was not a fit. I talked with Simone about the proper allocation of human resources and told her I was a square peg in a round hole.

I felt the best solution for me and the company was to resign as president of the division, and become a part-time adviser to Simone and the new division president. This would remove me from day-to-day operations, yet allow me to contribute to the success of the division. Simone promoted Ed Resendez, who was Kinecta's chief credit officer, to president of the Nix Check Cashing Division.

I resigned from Kinecta in July 2009. The strategic sale of Nix Check Cashing to Kinecta did not play out exactly as I had envisioned, but it was far better than selling to a competitor, and I am proud of this accomplishment. I continue to wish Kinecta and Nix Check Cashing (now called Nix Financial) the very best, and hope they achieve tremendous success.

I have never been interested in full retirement and was terrified that I might be miserably unhappy, but it's been wonderful! It took me a number of months to adjust to the reality that I was no longer connected to Nix Check Cashing in any way. Our company had been a huge part of my life and was my favorite hobby. I enjoyed being part of an incredible team of people, and I loved the challenge of creating and maintaining a successful business that made me proud. I expected that I would have been associated with Nix Check Cashing in some way on a part-time basis for many years to come, but it didn't play out that way. I, of course, wrote an affirmation to help me adopt the proper mindset:

"I am so excited to be retired with the freedom, time, money, energy, health, and enthusiasm to do whatever I want, when I want, free of worry, stress, and business obligations."

I have found many new joys in life. My favorite thing to do is spend time with my twin grandsons Timmy and Tommy. They love hanging out with Papa and Grammy, and we do simple fun things together. This is a joy that I didn't have or take time to do with my own kids. We had a great family and I spent whatever free time I had with them, but I worked hard and was gone a lot, and I missed the simple joys of watching them grow up. I'm thrilled now to have the time to spend with my grandsons. We are blessed to have a wonderful family.

Pam and I spend a lot of time talking, and we look forward to dinner and spending the evening together. But we also each go about our own business during the day. As they say, "I married you for better or for worse, but not for lunch." It's good.

We enjoy spending time on our sailboat, and spend about half the summer together on our boat in Catalina each year. I'm so lucky Pam loves the boat and is my best friend. Pam used to call me "the Ant Man," because I had to be doing something all of the time. She would say, "Just relax and enjoy yourself," but I couldn't. Retiring forced me to develop a new skill set: I can now sit on my butt and enjoy my surroundings and life for extended periods of time. This has brought new kinds of joy to my life. I have also found a new sense of appreciation for my friends and family, something that was hard for me to realize when I was busy and sometimes consumed with my work responsibilities. I am also thrilled to have time for an excellent excercise and stretching program. I highly recommend reading the book *Younger Next Year: A Guide to living like 50 until you're 80 and beyond* by Chris Crowley & Henry S. Lodge, M.D.

I served on the Board of Directors of A Better L.A. for the past five years, and continue to support this terrific nonprofit organization founded by former USC football coach and current coach of the NFL Seahawks, Pete Carroll. A Better L.A. is making a big difference in the low-income areas of Los Angeles, and is at the forefront of a new approach to solving the challenge of violence, its root causes, and its domino impact in the inner city. ABLA funds, trains, and empowers outreach workers, from within their own communities, to keep our kids safe. Its workers teach over 170 life-skills workshops, make over 150 social service referrals, take over 600 kids on field trips, connect over 800 kids to sports, informally mentor over 1,200 youth, and engage over 50,000 kids and families each year. ABLA has achieved extraordinary results, including greatly reduced homicides: 70 percent and 42 percent drops in our two main target areas.

I was also on the Board of Directors of the Los Angeles County Sheriff's Youth Foundation from 2000 to 2008. We directed dozens of community programs that were very effective in helping underprivileged and at-risk kids.

I continue to serve on the advisory board of William and Henry Associates, which is Dave Ianinni's investment banking firm, and on the board of the Catalina Island Yacht Club.

Many of my friends are retired, and we all agree that for some unexplainable reason, we are busy and having lots of fun. The question we ask ourselves is: "How did we ever have enough time to work?" I can wholeheartedly recommend retirement as long as you have the ability to stay busy with something you enjoy. It doesn't have to be work!

The following article ran in the *New York Times Magazine* on November 7, 2008, while I was working at Kinecta. It describes very clearly what we were hoping to accomplish, and everything we were up against. – TN

Check Cashers, Redeemed
By Douglas McGray

The lobby of the Nix Check Cashing outlet on South Figueroa and West Imperial, in the Watts neighborhood of south Los Angeles, was bright and loose. Twenty or so people, black and Latino, dressed in jeans and T-shirts or sport jerseys or work uniforms, stood in a line that snaked back from a long row of bulletproof cashiers' windows all the way to the front door. The room was loud, in a friendly way; everyone seemed to be talking with everyone else. Every once in a while, all together, the line would erupt into raucous laughter.

"Next customer," said a cashier, Joseph, a young black guy with a sweet, quiet manner. He wore black sneakers, black Dickies and a white polo shirt with a Nix logo — a retail uniform.

The customer at the window next to Joseph's looked over her shoulder. "Sister!" she yelled. "Next in line!"

It didn't feel like a bank.

Twenty or thirty years ago, traditional financial institutions fled neighborhoods like Watts, and guys like Tom Nix, co-founder of the biggest chain of check cashers and payday lenders in Southern California, rushed into the vacuum. They built a whole new financial subculture, which now includes regional giants like Nix, national brands like Ace Cash Express, Advance America and Check 'n Go and thousands of local chains and anonymous corner stores — more outlets, in total, than all the McDonald's restaurants in the United States plus all the Starbucks coffee shops. Inside, it's like banking turned upside down. Poor customers are commodities, deposits are irrelevant, bad credit makes for a good loan candidate and recessions can be boom times. Add up all those small transactions and throw in businesses like pawnshops and auto-title lenders, and you've got a big industry — $100 billion annually and growing. Nix alone pulled in $28 million in fees last year.

"Next customer," Joseph said. A guy slid his paycheck and a Nix ID card under the window. Joseph stamped the check, placed it under a gunmetal contraption called a photoscope, next to the ID card, and pulled a lever, thunk, which snapped a picture of the man, his ID and his check on a single negative. Then he counted out 20s. "Do you want to pay any bills today?" Joseph asked. "You get five free money orders with that."

There are two big problems with businesses like Nix Check Cashing. One is that the fees are high. Most cashers pocket between 2 and 4 percent of each check's value, which a recent Brookings Institution study calculated could add up to $40,000 in fees over a customer's working life. And their version of credit, a two- or four-week cash advance against a postdated check, known as a payday loan, is even pricier — about 30 times the annualized interest rate of a typical credit card.

The second problem is that cashing your paycheck, instead of depositing it, encourages you to spend all your money rather than saving whatever is left over at the end of the month. (Down the counter, a pair of young black women in tight, bright tops looked around a bit nervously as a cashier counted out thousands in small bills. "It's tax-refund time," the cashier told me as the women walked out.)

But it's also true that traditional banks are far from blameless, especially where low-income customers are concerned, and check cashers and payday lenders do get some important things right. "If they're properly regulated and scrutinized, there's nothing wrong with check cashing as a concept and there's nothing wrong with payday loans as a concept," Robert L. Gnaizda, general counsel for the Greenlining Institute, a California nonprofit focused on financial services and civil rights, told me. "And there's nothing automatically good about free checking accounts if you have multiple fees whenever you make the most minor mistake."

Today's financial crisis has many origins. But here's one cause that is often overlooked: Traditional bankers badly misread the market for financial services in low-to-moderate-income communities. "Banks have been approaching these customers purely from a short-term-gain perspective, and they've missed opportunities," Matt Fellowes, director of the Pew Safe Banking Opportunities Project, told me. Banks declined to offer small, simple lines of credit to poor and blue-collar customers, leaving them to payday lenders, while they pushed high-limit, high-interest credit cards on everyone and acquired hundreds of billions in subprime debt. They undervalued the hundreds of billions a year in modest paychecks that pass through a place like Nix and ended up short on cash. Now that the economy has turned ugly, these poor and blue-collar customers are the hardest-squeezed. Payday loans are up, Nix told me when I spoke to him recently, and check-cashing revenue is down.

Legislators around the country have identified savings as a way to shore up low-income communities and expand the middle class. There are a few significant bills before Congress, and more at the state level, that would help poor and working-class families save money — like increasing the amount welfare recipients are allowed to sock away before the system cuts off their benefits. But some 28 million Americans still go without a bank account, including more than 20 percent of Latino and African-American households, and more than 50 million have no credit score, which means no access to mainstream credit. These are the people in line at Nix.

A number of city and state governments have announced moratoriums on new check-cashing stores or set a ceiling on their fees. Fifteen states, including New York, have either outlawed payday lending or capped interest rates low enough to make it a money loser. And in 2006, Congress effectively banned payday loans to military personnel anywhere in the country. At the same time, lawmakers have tried to nudge banks toward low-income customers. By the end of the year, in the biggest effort yet, Gov. Arnold Schwarzenegger of California plans to announce the roll-out of an initiative called Bank on California — a concept piloted in 2006 in San Francisco, where the mayor's office persuaded banks to relax their standards, and in some cases their fees, for new account holders in exchange for a free marketing push from the city in poor neighborhoods. Officials from several other states, interested in copying the idea, will visit California for the kickoff, and more than three dozen cities, including Seattle, Los Angeles and Savannah, Ga., are already drawing up their own versions.

But while regulation has curbed some of the worst excesses of the alternative financial-services industry and made mainstream banking more accessible, there remains a big gap between those worlds. As C. K. Prahalad, the economist and author of "The Fortune at the Bottom of the Pyramid," told me, "We don't think enough about how to migrate from one to the other in a sensible way." Check cashers and payday lenders want to keep their customers, and banks tend to be ambivalent about luring them away or unsure how to do it.

Tom Nix's life, and his work, is the story of how we got here, to a separate and mostly unequal financial industry for the poor. But it may also be the story of a new way out. Last fall, Nix sold his entire chain for $45 million to one of the country's largest credit unions, Kinecta, which turned around and gave him an unlikely assignment: Put a credit-union window in every Nix store and help Kinecta take mainstream banking services to some of L.A.'s poorest neighborhoods — by thinking less like a bank and more like a check casher.

"They're absolutely blazing a new path," says Jennifer Tescher, director of the Center for Financial Services Innovation, a nonprofit research group affiliated with Chicago's Shore Bank. "They bought the chain wholesale and then kept Tom Nix as an executive, which in many ways is very smart." A few banks and credit unions have tried retail check-cashing start-ups, or arm's-length partnerships with existing check cashers, but they've come at the industry as outsiders. Bankers were always in charge. Or they operated on a comparatively small scale. Nix Check Cashing carries a million customers in its database.

"I've always wanted to vilify check cashers," says Elwood Hopkins, a consultant working with the L.A. mayor's office on the city's version of a Bank on California scheme. "And this is in no way a defense of the fees. But I think financial institutions have a lot to learn from them."

Tom Nix is tall and trim with short gray hair, narrow-set eyes and faintly ruddy skin. He has a 40-foot boat he likes to sail off Catalina Island, and the sticker on the bumper of his new Lexus says that that's what he'd rather be doing. He wears a conservative suit, a banker's suit, even for ambling around Compton and Watts, which he does like a small-town mayor, greeting everyone who passes by.

"How you doing?" he said, nodding, as we passed a young black guy in a baggy Sixers jersey that hung down to his knees. Nix is white; most of his customers are not.

Nix got into check cashing by accident. His dad, Tom Nix Sr., managed a fleet of drivers who delivered bread door to door, the way the milkman delivered milk. By the 1960s, delivery was a dying business, but at the warehouse in south L.A. where Nix's drivers loaded their trucks, locals, mostly poor, mostly black, would come around to buy day-old bread. So Nix's father started selling groceries out of the warehouse.

Nix took me to see the old store. Now it's called Pancho Grande. A mural of the Virgin Mary, in bright hues, stands taller than the door. The neighborhood, once almost entirely black, is now mostly Latino, Nix explained, a shift that happened across south L.A. as immigrants came up from Mexico and black families left for the inland suburbs. When the Nix store was here, mom-and-pop grocery stores and liquor places usually cashed checks free. But between bad checks and bounced checks, shopkeepers in the neighborhood lost money, even though they would turn away people who looked risky — whatever risky looked like to them. So in the early 1970s, Nix Jr., who had become his father's part-ner, made a photo ID for their customers and ordered his first photoscope, then an arcane new security tool. Soon

Nix was cashing checks for anyone who walked in, doing it fast and cutting the family's losses. "People lined up down these stairs," he said, pointing to the store's office at the back. "All the way down the center aisle and out to the sidewalk."

For most of the 20th century, banking was a protected business. If you wanted to open a new bank, you had to go before a board of regulators and prove you wouldn't provide competition that would threaten an existing bank in the neighborhood. In exchange for a captive market, banks had to abide by strict rules. But in the mid- 1970s, regulators started to allow more competition. Banks had to pay closer attention to their profits and their losses. Suddenly, Nix's local bank began charging him a fee to deposit checks into his commercial account. Nix realized he either had to stop cashing checks for people or start charging them for the service.

"We charged a dime at first," Nix recalled. "People got mad, they left, but in a couple months, business returned. Then we charged 35 cents. Same thing happened. Then we started to charge 1 percent. We began to realize this might be a business."

In 1978, Nix leased an old gas station in Watts and built it into what looked like a tiny, stripped-down bank. He called it Nix Check Cashing. A year later, he was cashing a million dollars in checks each week. Then in

1980, Congress began to deregulate the banking industry. Branches sprouted in rich neighborhoods, where they battled one another for the wealthiest depositors, and they shut down in poor and working-class neighborhoods. Where they remained, they introduced new fees for customers who kept little in their accounts for the bank to invest. Around the country, the check-cashing business boomed. Nix opened new stores as fast as he could raise capital. Any place the banks neglected, that was the real estate he wanted. By the end of the 1980s, Nix had grown big enough to get name-checked by the Beastie Boys: "I'm charming and dashing/I'm rental-car bashing/Phony-paper passing/At Nix Check Cashing."

"That's name recognition!" Nix told me with a smile.

Times have changed, somewhat. Today more than 90 percent of check cashers and payday lenders sit within a mile of a bank, according to a recent Brookings Institution report. It's no longer primarily geography, in other words, that is keeping banks and poor customers apart. "Banks aren't shying away from low- and moderate-income neighborhoods," says Fellowes, the report's author. But, he added, "they're not going after the opportunity in an informed-enough manner to be very successful."

The first thing you notice when you walk in the door at Nix is a list of products, services and prices, a bit like a fast-food menu. Some of the prices are quite high, but the charges are neither confusing nor deceptive. "They're going to charge you $13, is that O.K.?" a cashier — young, Latina, long blond hair, long pink nails — asked as a bulky, middle-aged guy handed over a stack of cash to send via Moneygram.

Even the payday loans are transparent. "Your max is $150, so make it out for $172.50," the cashier Joseph told a stocky black woman in a baseball cap, standing at the counter with an open checkbook. (Unlike check-cashing customers, payday borrowers are by necessity bank customers — they have to write a postdated check to get a loan.) The woman was paying a lot — $22.50 to borrow $150 for just two weeks. But there were no surprises, no hidden fees.

Compare that with what a lot of banks do. Bank of America took heat earlier this year for more than doubling the interest rate on some credit-card accounts, even if the cardholder pays every bill on time. Banks, meanwhile, have nearly quadrupled their fee income in the last decade, according to the F.D.I.C., while credit-card late charges and over-limit charges have nearly tripled. Fees imposed on customers for temporarily overdrawing their accounts — by accident or on purpose — have been particularly lucrative; banks made $25.3 billion in 2006 on overdraft-related fees, up 48 percent in two years, according to the Center for Responsible Lending. On the Web site of

Strunk and Associates, a big seller of overdraft programs, bank and credit-union executives offer glowing testimonials. "Strunk's program has exceeded expectations," one writes. "We have generated a 100 percent increase in overdraft revenue."

Some customers choose Nix over a bank because it is cheaper than paying overdraft fees. For others, it's convenient. Some go to Nix because check cashing is what they know. Others go because they live in communities where nobody takes a check or a card, not even the landlord, and cash machines are scarce. Still others go because they always seem to have a Final Notice in the bill stack, and they can't wait a week or longer for a paycheck to clear — that includes a lot of people with a bank account somewhere.

But there are less-obvious factors too. Nix hires from the neighborhood and pays well enough that cashiers stick around. Word spreads, and in Watts or Highland Park or Pacoima, that reputation often carries more weight than some bank ad on a bus stop. "It's social marketing 101," says Hopkins, the consultant.

I frequently saw cashiers address customers by name and ask about family or friends in common. One customer asked if the manager could come over, then broke the news that her husband had passed away. "What happened?" the manager gasped. Then, shaking her head: "He always came in with his pennies." And Nix dresses up branches less formally than banks do — no suits, no office furniture, no carpeting — so a construction worker can show up straight from his shift, in dirty clothes, and, Nix says, not feel out of place.

Nix's cashiers also try to never say no. Take photo identification. A lot of customers don't have a driver's license. Nix stores have accepted high-school yearbooks. They've been known to cash a McDonald's paycheck if someone comes in wearing a McDonald's uniform. They even have a phone in the lobby, so a cashier can call a customer's job site and then patch the customer in, listen to him talk to his supervisor and decide if they sound like a legitimate boss and employee. Nix says he loses as much as 5 percent of his check-cashing revenue on bad checks, but it's worth it, he says, to be known as a place that says yes.

I met Oscar Enriquez leaving the Nix branch in Highland Park, a working-class area near Pasadena. He was skinny and just shy of middle age, with a quick grin and tattoos down his sunburned forearms. Enriquez worked in the neighborhood as a street cleaner; he picks up trash and scrubs graffiti. The job paid about $425 a week, he told me, a good chunk of which he wired to his wife, who has been living in Mississippi and taking care of her ailing mother. He told me he tries to avoid debt whenever he can. "If I don't have money, I wait until the next payday," he said firmly. "That's it." But he pays a fee to cash his paychecks. Then he pays even more to send a Moneygram to his wife. There's a bank, just down the street, that could do those things free. I asked him why he didn't take his business there.

"Oh, man, I won't work with them no more," Enriquez explained. "They're not truthful."

Two years ago, Enriquez opened his first bank account. "I said I wanted to start a savings account," he said. He thought the account was free, until he got his first statement. "They were charging me for checks!" he said, still upset about it. "I didn't want checks. They're always charging you fees. For a while, I didn't use the bank at all, they charged like $100 in fees." Even studying his monthly statements, he couldn't always figure out why they charged what they charged. Nix is almost certainly more expensive, but it's also more predictable and transparent, and that was a big deal to Enriquez.

Marlo Lopez had no broad gripe with banks, but his experience was similar. He moved to the United States from Peru a couple of years ago (with a visa) and got a job as a mechanic at a food-processing plant. Lopez opened his first bank account last summer. A couple of months later, out for dinner, he overdrew his account by 18 cents and got hit with a $35 penalty. It was his fault, he said; he thought he had more in the account than he did. Still, losing that money all at once unsettled him. He kept the account but returned to cashing his checks at Nix.

In the spring of 2007, Nix was working hard to unload his business. He had actually been trying to sell his chain to a bank for more than a decade, and now he was running out of time. He was about to turn 60, and he thought he owed his family (and his investors) an exit. Nix wanted to sell high to a responsible bank, retire well and be a hero, the guy who took real banking to L.A.'s poorest neighborhoods. But the most likely buyer was another check-cashing chain. Nix was prepared to do the deal, but it was not how he dreamed of going out.

Then Kinecta Federal Credit Union called with its offer. "We were trying to understand why check cashers have been successful in underserved areas where banks haven't," Kinecta's president and C.E.O., Simone Lagomarsino, told me. What they concluded was that most banks simply didn't know low-income neighborhoods or understand them. "We go in with this cookie-cutter approach: This is our branch, this is our way we do business," she says.

As Nix and Lagomarsino negotiated the sale, he encouraged her to make it easier for his customers to open a bank account. At most banks, if you've bounced too many checks, you're banned for five to seven years. Lagomarsino agreed to reduce that limbo period to one year. Next she realized she would need to deal with the most controversial part of Nix's business, the payday loans. At first, she told me, "I assumed we wouldn't do them." Nix actually felt the same way, once. In the late 1980s, when a few check cashers started to accept postdated personal checks and advance cash for a fee, Nix thought it was a sleazy scheme. He thought so even after California legalized the practice in 1997. "I didn't want to be a loan shark," he told me. "But the reality is, customers wanted it."

He told Lagomarsino why. A bounced check, a fee to reconnect a utility, a late-payment fee on your credit card, or an underground loan, any of those things can cost more than a payday loan. And then there are overdraft charges. "Banks, credit unions, we've been doing payday loans, we just call it something different," Lagomarsino says. "When it starts to get used like a payday loan, it's worse."

The payday borrowers I met at Nix were a complex group. There was Johnny Bravo, an ex-marine, now a harried delivery driver. ("I'm not even supposed to be here," he said, rushing back to his truck with a fold of bills.) He told me he gets a payday loan every other Friday, pretty much without fail. Sometimes he needs it for bills. Sometimes it's for gas — he owns a big, thirsty S.U.V. But mostly he described the loan as cash to enjoy his weekend.

"How much do you think you spend a year on payday loans?" I asked.

"Well, finance is about 45 dollars; add that up . . . ," he

said, and paused. "Comes out to a pretty good chunk of change," he admitted. "But I don't think of it that way."

Bravo is exactly the kind of case consumer advocates bring up when they call for a ban on payday loans. But for better or worse, the guy loves Nix. "They treat me with respect, they're really nice," he said. He's especially fond of the manager, Beatriz. She grew up in the neighborhood and has worked at Nix for almost 20 years now.

Then there was Carlos Garcia. He got out of the military, got some credit cards and got in trouble. It took him a few years to pay off his debt. Now he's careful, but money is still tight. He usually works two full-time jobs, and he earns enough for himself. He has a couple of brothers, though, who have been out of work, and he has his mother to help look after. That takes him to Nix a few times a year for a loan. But he's strategic. "I get it because I want to make a payment on time," he said. He does the math, he told me, and borrows only when the fee for a small loan will cost less than the penalty for a late car payment or an overdraft charge.

As different as they are when it comes to money, Garcia and Bravo agreed on one thing: "I don't use credit cards," Bravo said. "I don't want to get into debt." That may sound crazy coming from a guy who spends more than $1,000 a year to borrow a thin stack of 20s over and over, but he had a point. It may be hard, some months, to pay off a $255 payday loan. But credit cards can get you into more serious trouble; credit-card debt can add up fast and linger for years.

Kinecta's executives decided to keep the payday loan and change the terms. Starting with three stores in the spring, and eventually across the entire chain, Nix is increasing the maximum loan from $255 to $400. They are dropping the fee from 18 percent ($45 for a two-week $255 loan) to 15 percent ($60 for a two-week $400 loan). And they will rebate a third more ($20, in the case of a $400 loan) into a savings account, after six months, if you pay your loans back and don't bounce any checks. People get payday loans because they have no savings, Lagomarsino explained. After six months, heavy payday borrowers will accumulate a small balance. Enough, she and Nix say they hope, to convince them they can afford to save more. Later, they say, they intend to drop fees further for borrowers who always pay back on time.

Once Kinecta finishes rolling out its new payday loans, Lagomarsino has promised to open Nix's books to outside researchers and publish data on its profits and losses. In the meantime, Kinecta will be under enormous scrutiny. "Some people said, 'Why does it have to be so visible?'" Lagomarsino told me, and laughed. "One or two branches wouldn't make a difference. This is the beauty of buying Nix. They were the largest alternative financial-services company in Southern California. If they change their fee structure, everyone has to change."

At the Nix Check Cashing in Highland Park, one of Kinecta's first credit-union windows opened at the end of April. It's a tiny branch, squeezed into a strip mall, a few storefronts down from a slummier-looking check casher and across the parking lot from an Advance America branch. By the door, a hand-drawn whiteboard advertised free checking and savings accounts. Inside, customers had to pass through a gantlet of Kinecta signs ("free," "we're all about convenience") to reach the check-cashing windows. Then, whenever someone slipped a check across the counter (or bought a bus pass, or mobile-phone minutes, or a prepaid debit card), Nix tellers asked if they'd like to open a free savings or checking account with a $5 deposit.

I expected mostly brushoffs. But people had questions. Lots of them, actually. (What's a credit union? Are there fees? What's the minimum balance? Can I deposit my checks at Nix for free?) Often people started in with the questions as soon as they got to the window, before the cashiers got around to a sales pitch. That doesn't mean they all signed up. Most of them didn't. But several did, and very few rejected the idea outright.

When I visited Nix in his new office at Kinecta, he seemed optimistic about the new business. "I've been trying to do this banking thing for more than 15 years," he said. "If we do it, the rest of the industry copies us." But, he said, "It has to be a viable business model."

Nix's definition of "viable" means some public criticism is bound to follow him to Kinecta. Even after knocking more than 30 percent off the fees, Nix's payday loans are still expensive, and Nix says he hopes to issue more of them, not fewer, because Nix stores will be cheaper than the competition. The fees are still astronomical, and more troubling, right now the average borrower at Nix takes out seven loans a year — with fees than can equal an annualized interest rate of 312 percent. "Any form of credit can be abused," Nix said when I asked him about the problem of repeat customers. "There's the guy who gets five credit cards. For some reason, it's O.K. when it's a mainstream product. There's a double standard."

It's going to take a lot of $20 rebates from Nix before someone with a payday-loan problem would accumulate any real savings. I asked Nix if he would consider advertising to these customers, straight out, that payday loans are bad for them. What about check-cashing customers who, out of habit, resist the idea of signing up for a bank account that would save them money?

"The last thing I want to tell someone who's been my customer for 20 years is, 'You've been a fool for 20 years, you never should have been coming in,'" Nix said, with a sudden edge in his voice. "I want to create choice."

Selling to the poor is a tricky business. Poor people pay more for just about everything, from fresh groceries to banking; Prahalad, the economist, calls it the "poverty penalty." They pay more for all kinds of reasons, but maybe most of all because mainstream firms decline to compete for their business. Nix has served customers that traditional financial institutions neglected, but he has also profited from that neglect. Whether he profited too much, charging poor communities what the market would bear — that's a moral question as much as an economic one. And there's no simple answer.

Not everyone is ready to trust Nix's motives just yet, or to embrace him as a champion of the poor, especially consumer advocates who have spent years lobbying to cap check-cashing and payday-loan rates and remember when Nix charged even more than he does today. "It behooves predatory companies like Nix to be seen positively by their communities," says Roberto Barragan, president of the Valley Economic Development Center and a critic of Nix from way back. "But at the end of the day, it's not about the financial well-being of his customers."

For now, most banks remain reluctant to fight with check cashers and payday lenders for low-income customers; they don't believe there's enough in it for them. Just a few years ago, though, wire-transfer companies like Western Union were the only option for immigrants who wanted to send money abroad. Banks thought it was a sketchy business. The transfer companies charged about the same as a payday loan, $15 to send $100 to Latin America. But then a few banks decided to compete with them, even accepting foreign ID cards. And then banks started to compete with one another. And pretty soon, just about every bank wired money overseas. Businesses like Western Union had to slash their fees by nearly two-thirds.

"These communities spend about $11 billion a year on ghettoized financial services, about the same as what Wall Street spends on mergers-and-acquisitions fees," says John Hope Bryant, founder of the nonprofit Operation Hope. "We're not talking about small change. But there's no competition for these dollars." That's the idea behind plans like Bank on California: to convince banks that marketing themselves to poor customers isn't just a charitable act; it's a benefit to the bottom line.

Nix says he hopes his model will do the same thing. "We're going to be a tough competitor," he told me. "We're going to get a lot of business, and that's going to force the rest of the industry to take a look at their prices, to be able to compete." It's not how you expect a banker to the poor to talk. But he might be onto something.

TOM NIX PHOTOS

(*Left to right*) Tom's grammar school picture, 1955. Tom the day after his liquor store fight, 1963

(*Above*) Tom giving a speech to the student body at the San Pedro High School pep rally, 1965.

(*Right*) Tom and Pam on the senior day sack race, 1966

(*Above*) A Tom Phillips painting of the Essex club house and members as it was in 1966. Tom and Pam are standing in front of his lowered 1959 Chevy

(*Above*) The Sheriff Academy class. Tom is the last man on the right, 1976.

(*Above*) The Nix family portrait. Tom with his wife Pam, and their two children
Billy and Tommy, 1983

(*Top*) The first Nix Check Cashing location to open, 1978

(*Above*) Tom's mom and dad standing at the drive-thru window of the first Nix location, 1978

(*Above*) The inside of a typical Nix Check Cashing location, 1989

(*Above*) Typical Nix Check Cashing location, 1989

THE  ® SYSTEM

- Simple, proven, safe, affordable
- Computerized point-of-sale system
- Automatic system-wide alerts & safeguards
- Minimizes bad checks
- Minimizes shortages
- Nix money orders
- Computerized money order system
- Wide range of financial services
- Professional support team

From a Sole Proprietorship to a National Chain a NIX Check Cashing® Center can boost Your Sales.

(*Above*) Nix brochure of store-within-a store business model, 1993

(*Above*) Annual food drive hosted by Nix Check Cashing. "The Union Bank of Nix" team. From left to right: Tom Nix; Thom Branch; Yolanda Brown; Richard Yee; Randy Dotemoto; Helen Shoemo, team member; Darline Gavin; Chris Vitale; Dora Cano; Michelle Esteem; Ricky Floyd, team member; Katrina Minor; Rick Hartnack, 2000

(*Above*) Rick Hartnack and Tom having their last breakfast at Norms, 2005

(*Above*) Los Angeles City Councilmen Bernard Parks, and Herb Wesson present Tom and Pam with a certificate, commemorating Nix Check Cashing's 40 years of excellent service, 2006

(*Above*) 1990s' billboard campaign (featuring Tom's wife, Pam, the blonde in the middle). Our slogan "Bank on Nix" became a reality when Kinecta Federal Credit Union purchased Nix Check Cashing on August 14, 2007.

(*Above*) Management Team picture celebrating 40 years of business